Liturgy as a Way
of Life

THE CHURCH   *James K. A. Smith, series editor*
AND POSTMODERN   www.churchandpomo.org
CULTURE

The Church and Postmodern
Culture series features high-profile
theorists in continental philosophy
and contemporary theology
writing for a broad, nonspecialist
audience interested in the impact of
postmodern theory on the faith and
practice of the church.

Also available in the series

Merold Westphal, *Whose Community? Which Interpretation? Philosphical Hermeneutics for the Church*

James K. A. Smith, *Who's Afraid of Postmodernism? Taking Derrida, Lyotard, and Foucault to Church*

John D. Caputo, *What Would Jesus Deconstruct? The Good News of Postmodernism for the Church*

Carl Raschke, *GloboChrist: The Great Commission Takes a Postmodern Turn*

Graham Ward, *The Politics of Discipleship: Becoming Post-material Citizens*

Daniel M. Bell Jr., *The Economy of Desire: Christianity and Capitalism in a Postmodern World*

Liturgy as a Way of Life

*Embodying the Arts in
Christian Worship*

Bruce Ellis Benson

Baker Academic
a division of Baker Publishing Group
Grand Rapids, Michigan

Published by Baker Academic
a division of Baker Publishing Group
P.O. Box 6287, Grand Rapids, MI 49516-6287
www.bakeracademic.com

Printed in the United States of America

Library of Congress Cataloging-in-Publication Data
Benson, Bruce Ellis, 1960–
    Liturgy as a way of life : embodying the arts in Christian worship / Bruce Ellis
Benson.
        p.   cm. — (The church and postmodern culture)
    Includes bibliographical references and index.
    ISBN 978-0-8010-3135-9 (pbk.)
    1. Worship. 2. Liturgics. 3. Christianity and art. 4. Christianity and the arts.
  5. Liturgy and art. 6. Liturgy and the arts. 7. Postmodernism—Religious aspects–
Christianity. I. Title.
BV15.B435 2013
246—dc23   2012031875

The internet addresses, email addresses, and phone numbers in this book are accurate at the time of publication. They are provided as a resource. Baker Publishing Group does not endorse them or vouch for their content or permanence.

In keeping with biblical principles of creation stewardship, Baker Publishing Group advocates the responsible use of our natural resources. As a member of the Green Press Initiative, our company uses recycled paper when possible. The text paper of this book is composed in part of post-consumer waste.

13 14 15 16 17 18 19   7 6 5 4 3 2 1

Contents

Series Preface

Current discussions in the church—from emergent "postmodern" congregations to mainline "missional" congregations—are increasingly grappling with philosophical and theoretical questions related to postmodernity. In fact, it could be argued that developments in postmodern theory (especially questions of "post-foundationalist" epistemologies) have contributed to the breakdown of former barriers between evangelical, mainline, and Catholic faith communities. Postliberalism—a related "effect" of postmodernism—has engendered a new, confessional ecumenism wherein we find nondenominational evangelical congregations, mainline Protestant churches, and Catholic parishes all wrestling with the challenges of postmodernism and drawing on the culture of postmodernity as an opportunity for rethinking the shape of our churches.

This context presents an exciting opportunity for contemporary philosophy and critical theory to "hit the ground," so to speak, by allowing high-level work in postmodern theory to serve the church's practice—including all the kinds of congregations and communions noted above. The goal of this series is to bring together high-profile theorists in continental philosophy and contemporary theology to write for a broad, nonspecialist audience interested in the impact of postmodern theory on the faith and practice of the church. Each book in the series will, from different angles and with different questions, undertake to answer questions such as, What does postmodern theory have to say about the shape of the church? How should concrete, in-the-pew and on-the-ground religious practices be impacted by postmodernism? What should the church look like in postmodernity? What has Paris to do with Jerusalem?

The series is ecumenical not only with respect to its ecclesial destinations but also with respect to the facets of continental philosophy and theory that are represented. A wide variety of theoretical commitments will be included, ranging from deconstruction to Radical Orthodoxy, including voices from Badiou to Žižek and the usual suspects in between (Nietzsche, Heidegger, Levinas, Derrida, Foucault, Irigaray, Rorty, and others). Insofar as postmodernism occasions a retrieval of ancient sources, these contemporary sources will be brought into dialogue with Augustine, Irenaeus, Aquinas, and other resources. Drawing on the wisdom of established scholars in the field, the series will provide accessible introductions to postmodern thought with the specific aim of exploring its impact on ecclesial practice. The books are offered, one might say, as French lessons for the church.

Series Editor's Foreword

JAMES K. A. SMITH

When philosophers and theologians engage postmodernism, they tend to spend their time debating arcane matters of epistemology, hermeneutics, and metanarratives. Meanwhile, a kind of "practical" postmodernism has emerged in the contemporary church in other, more tangible ways. One can read the renewal of the arts in the church—including new concerns about the arts in worship—as evidence that Christianity's complicity with modernity might be waning, at least in some respects.

Over the past couple of centuries, the church's worship—perhaps especially in Protestant evangelicalism—unwittingly mimicked the rationalism (and dualism) of modernity. Assuming with Descartes that humans are primarily "thinking things," worship has been centered on didactic teaching. A few songs merely function as a preface to a long sermon, the goal of which is the dissemination of information to brains-on-a-stick, sitting on their hands. The body has no role in such worship; it is worship for the proverbial brains-in-a-vat of philosophical fame. And because the body has no essential role in such worship, there is also no place for the arts, which are inherently sensible, even sensual. One can sense this in the pragmatism of church architecture, or the stark minimalism of interior design in Protestant churches, where the only adornment was often scriptural texts emblazoned on the walls. In rationalist worship spaces, even the wallpaper is didactic.

Such "rationalist" worship also tends to not have any real place for the Eucharist. Indeed, I think one can generally note a correlation between the centrality of the Eucharist in worship and an appreciation for the materiality that underwrites the arts. So what's lost in modernity and our unwitting adoption of rationalism is just the sort of sacramentality that undergirds Christian affirmation of the body—the same sensibility that values the arts. The metaphysics of modernity flattens the world, reducing human persons to information processors.[1] And if we buy into this, we will "worship" accordingly. The didactic will trump the affective; the intellect will crowd out the imagination; the body will be present as only a vehicle to get the mind in the pew. Welcome to the cathedral of Descartes.

But just as evangelicals are rediscovering the sacramental imagination that is carried in the liturgical tradition, they are also beginning to appreciate the importance of the arts—in culture and in worship. Both of these trends, I would suggest, are the fruit of our discomfort with the rationalist model and testify to its implosion. As such, both developments are also a kind of postmodern critique *in practice*. To appreciate the arts is to appreciate that we are more than *thinking* things. To recover the arts is to remember that we have bodies—which is to remember what Christians knew well before modernity. So we are now seeing an explosion of centers, institutes, conferences, and books devoted to "arts and worship." More and more congregations are intentionally incorporating the arts into worship—including a range of forms, from visual art to liturgical dance, on top of an explosion of new music. Granted, much of this might simply function as ornamentation of a model that is still largely didactic and rationalist. But there is an intuition at work here that unsettles our modern habits.

So there is good reason to celebrate and affirm this newfound interest in the arts, particularly for those of us who have seen postmodernism as a kind of demodernizing discipline to help the church awake from its modern slumbers, thereby opened to recover the

---

1. For a diagnosis of this state of affairs and an invitation to recover a sacramental vision, see Hans Boersma's important book *Heavenly Participation: The Weaving of a Sacramental Tapestry* (Grand Rapids: Eerdmans, 2011).

ancient treasury of the church's formative practices. This is what Robert Webber described as an "ancient-future" sensibility: resources for a postmodern future found in the buried treasures of an ancient heritage.

In this book, Bruce Ellis Benson shares the same intuition about a link between liturgy and the arts (and vice versa). So one could hope that a new appreciation for the arts in the church might be a kind of sacramental "gateway drug" that draws congregations to liturgical renewal. Conversely, one could hope that those congregations that are intentionally recovering the rich panoply of the church's liturgical practices might thereby consider how the arts are characterized by the same affective imaginativity.

However, while a renewal of the arts can be read as a "practical postmodernism," we also need to be cautious. For the new emphasis on art, creativity, and imagination could just as easily be simply *another* modernism—a recovery of modern romanticism, even if that might be an implicit critique of Enlightenment rationalism. As Benson argues, romantic conceptions of art are still characterized by the hallmarks of modernity, particularly its atomism and emphasis on autonomy. The romantic notion of artistic creation is modern autonomy by other means: the artist as lone genius, as heroic creator, as independent inventer who creates virtually *ex nihilo*. Sound familiar? Yes, while we might applaud the romantic critique of Enlightenment rationalism, we should also be careful about what gets put in its place: a view of human creators that makes us tantamount to the Creator, even competitors of the Creator. We can unwittingly end up buying into this when we overplay any analogy between God's creative activity and our creativity. "We are not 'artists' in the strong sense that God is," Benson cautions. "Only God can bring forth creation from nothing." Indeed, "we are likely to go wrong in our thinking about ourselves as artists when we see ourselves as 'like' God." The cult of creativity can be just another way to supplant the Creator.

This is why Benson pushes back against those notions of creativity that idolize the heroic, creative genius and reduce art to the expression of subjectivity. This, he argues, is just another version of modern individualism, autonomy, and independence. (It is also a picture, I'd suggest, that plays right into the hands of what sociologist Christian Smith has described as the "moralistic therapeutic deism" that passes for Christianity in North America. "Making room for the arts" becomes just another way of making room for individual assertion and preference and taste.)

Thus Benson challenges the cult of creativity—and Christian "we-are-little-creators" rhetoric—and instead sketches a different paradigm for Christian affirmation of art: *improvisation*. Drawing on his expertise in hermeneutics and his experience as a jazz musician, Benson invites us to see artistic creation not as work of individual invention but as communal interaction. Artists don't create *ex nihilo*; they work with what's given to them. When we frame art as improvisation, he argues, we see that it exhibits the most basic structure of creaturely existence—the dynamic of call and response. Drawing on Jean-Louis Chrétien, Hans-Georg Gadamer, Jean-Luc Marion, and other continental theorists, Benson helps us to appreciate that improvisation is at the heart of discipleship because it is at the heart of being human.

Preface

This book has been many years in the making. It expresses my thinking not just about art and the church but about the very nature of our lives. There are so many people who helped to make this book possible that I am bound to leave someone out. First, I would like to acknowledge my debt to Hans-Georg Gadamer. As I have come to the conclusion of this project, I realize (once again) how indebted I am to him. His thought influences every page, and I am ever grateful not only for his friendship and mentoring but also for his encouragement when I was first formulating my ideas regarding improvisation. Let me next thank the hundreds of students who have been part of my Philosophy of the Arts course over the past twenty years. They have asked probing questions and forced me to think through these issues. My thanks also go to my colleagues in the Philosophy Department at Wheaton, who read portions of the manuscript and gave (as always) very constructive feedback. I have greatly benefited from numerous conversations with colleagues in the Art Department, the Conservatory, and the Theatre/Communications Department. The Wheaton College Alumni Association provided travel funds for this book, and I received release time that made the writing of this book possible. My thanks to my dean, Jill Peláez Baumgaertner, for her support. I wish to thank Jamie Smith, who invited me to write this book for his series and has provided excellent advice along the way. Thanks to Bob Hosack, who patiently awaited the completion of the manuscript. For continued

dialogue on the arts and theology—not to mention much encouragement—many thanks go to Jeremy Begbie. For dialogue on the
arts and philosophy, I am pleased to thank Nicholas Wolterstorff.
Artists who have read and commented on my work include Bruce
Herman and Ted Prescott. My conversation with Enrique Martínez
Celaya has been enlightening, and I am delighted to be involved in
his art foundation, Whale & Star. The art historian and erstwhile
museum curator Dan Siedell has provided invaluable and generous
feedback, not to mention inspiration, at various points along the
way. My thanks go to Jeremy Heuslein, who kindly read an earlier
version of the manuscript and provided helpful comments, and to
Peter Christensen for helping with the proofs. Peter Goodwin Heltzel
has provided many constructive suggestions. Thanks to John Walton
for his comments on creation and Genesis. Many thanks also to
Scott and Elizabeth Benson. I am grateful for conversations with
such artists and/or worship leaders as John Bayless, Daniel Bayless,
David Davis, Sanford Dole, Makoto Fujimura, Tom Jennings, Dan
Kimball, Brandon Muchow, Buddy Owens, Jimmy Owens, and
Jeff Warren. My visits to such churches as All Saint's Episcopal
Church (Beverly Hills), Redeemer Presbyterian Church (New York
City), Rock Harbor Church (Costa Mesa), Saddleback Church and
its conference for worship leaders (Lake Forest, California), Saint
Gregory of Nyssa Episcopal Church (San Francisco), Saint Peter's
Lutheran Church (New York City), Saint Sabina Roman Catholic
Church (Chicago), and Vintage Faith Church (Santa Cruz) have
been enormously helpful.

Just seeing that list will tip some readers off to the fact that
the folks and institutions I will be discussing as examples of artists, worship leaders, and churches vary. What I have discovered
in working on this book is that there are many churches that have
markedly differing worship styles and, as a result, are ministering
to markedly different people. Thanks be to God! As it turns out,
my own preference in worship is rather high-church Anglican/Epis-
copalian. Yet I hardly think that such worship is necessarily better
than all others, nor would I for a moment suggest that everyone
adopt it. Indeed, often when I attend other churches I think "this
is wonderful!"—even though I am delighted to return to my own
church the following Sunday. As becomes clear the more one attends
various churches, they have different qualities and worship styles
worth commending. Who one is and where one is on one's spiritual

journey have a great deal to do with which church one ultimately finds an appropriate fit. For myself, I can say that I learned far more than I could have ever expected from visiting a wide variety of churches and gained a deep appreciation for the Holy Spirit at work in many different settings.

Of course, having said all that, I must add the following regarding a fairly standard convention in writing a book. Although authors in "acknowledgment" sections often thank various people who helped them with the book, such thanks almost always conclude with something like "any mistakes, of course, remain my own." But why is it that we would only get *good* ideas from others and the bad ones always happen to be our own? It's like a reverse practice of insurance companies that call disasters "acts of God," as if God only gets credit for really bad things. Naturally, we don't actually believe in this standard author's reuse. It's really, as I've said, more of a convention. After all, you can't really say, "For all the stupid things I've said, so-and-so is equally to blame."

Yet that convention is upstaged by an even more interesting one—that *I* am the author of this book. Yes, my name's on the cover and the copyright is in my name, but that's also more convention than reality. Here I am not arguing for the classic "death of the author" idea propagated by Roland Barthes, who is perhaps best remembered for his famous statement that "the birth of the reader must be at the cost of the death of the author."[1] Thankfully, no one needs to die, in my view. Instead, as should become readily apparent to anyone who reads this book, I'm only the author of it to a certain degree. Lots of the ideas I work with are really "someone else's." To be sure, I do cite various people and even quote from them at points. But I'm really much more indebted to them than any citation, quotation, or acknowledgment section could ever make clear.

In an important sense, that's what this book is all about—that living (and not simply "making art") is a process of improvisation, in which one starts with things gifted to us by other people and works from there. Ultimately, I argue that this improvisational practice is best thought of as a kind of liturgy.

1. Roland Barthes, "The Death of the Author," in *Image, Music, Text*, trans. Stephen Heath (New York: Hill and Wang, 1977), 148. Of course, Barthes is hardly arguing that there are now to be no authors but merely that "authorship" in a strong sense (in which the author is solely in control of the meaning of her text) is neither desirable nor tenable.

I first began thinking about improvisation when I encountered the work of the phenomenologist Roman Ingarden, who wrote on (among other things) musical creation and performance. Although Ingarden provides a highly nuanced view, I began to realize that the model with which he was working simply failed to acknowledge how much improvisation is part of art.[2] Not long after my article on Ingarden was published, an Old Testament scholar friend of mine (Frans den Exter Blokland) who had read the article astutely responded by saying, "But isn't what you say about improvisation in music really what I am also doing in interpreting the Bible?" I told him that I thought he was quite right.[3] And I soon came to see that *life* is improvisational. Although I have worked out this improvisational aspect in regard to music,[4] here I want to expand on that work to speak not merely about art in general but life itself. As should become clear, *we are all improvisers in all that we do*.

Yet, if our very existence is improvisational, then this changes the way we think about what we do artistically and otherwise. In other words, it's not as if *I'm* the one lifting ideas from others and they all got theirs by way of the mystery of genius. T. S. Eliot—certainly one of the more innovative of poets—puts it rather bluntly: "One of the surest of tests [of quality] is the way in which a poet borrows. Immature poets imitate; mature poets steal."[5] The context for that quote is an essay on the playwright Philip Massinger, and it is quite clear that Eliot thinks that Massinger is an immature writer who merely *imitates* Shakespeare. Speaking of stealing, a quote often attributed to Pablo Picasso (also known for innovation) is, "Good

2. See Bruce Ellis Benson, "Roman Ingarden and the Problem of Jazz," *Tijdschrift voor Filosofie* 55 (1993): 677–93.

3. For an account of how biblical interpretation can be explained improvisationally, see Bruce Ellis Benson, "The Improvisation of Hermeneutics: Jazz Lessons for Interpreters," in *Hermeneutics at the Crossroads*, ed. Kevin J. Vanhoozer, James K. A. Smith, and Bruce Ellis Benson (Bloomington: Indiana University Press, 2006), and Benson, "Improvising Texts, Improvising Communities: Jazz, Heteronomy, and *Ekklēsia*," in *Resonant Witness: Conversations between Music and Theology*, ed. Jeremy S. Begbie and Steven Guthrie (Grand Rapids: Eerdmans, 2011).

4. See Bruce Ellis Benson, *The Improvisation of Musical Dialogue: A Phenomenology of Music* (Cambridge: Cambridge University Press, 2003).

5. T. S. Eliot, "Philip Massinger," in *The Sacred Wood*, 2nd ed. (London: Methuen, 1928), 125.

artists copy; great artists steal."[6] Whether Picasso knew he was stealing from Eliot is hard to say. After all, a common anonymous saying is, "He who is most creative conceals his sources the best." And, even before Eliot and Picasso, supposedly Benjamin Franklin said that "originality is the art of concealing your sources."[7] But Picasso clearly does admit to stealing: "When there's anything to steal, I steal."[8] What else would one expect from a great artist?

Not surprisingly, the view I take of my own authorship is one that I see as indicative of the creative process in general. I suggest that we think of ourselves as artistically improvising rather than creating. As we shall see, there is a very good theological basis for this way of thinking. On this point, though, I am not alone: others I cite throughout the book come very close to saying exactly that. Of course, I admit that this suggestion goes fundamentally against the grain of what most of us have been taught to think about artists and artistic creation, which we'll consider in the second chapter. That's also partly what this book is about—challenging what we think about art: what art *is* and exactly *who* makes art and *how* art is made. In short, I contend that we are *all* artists, that our very lives should be seen *as* art, and that we should live *liturgically* in service to God and neighbor.

Ultimately, my goal here is to explore the deep and interpenetrating relationship of life, art, and worship, though not with the intent of merely sketching some *theory* about their relationship. Instead, it is about working out *a way of life* that can properly be termed "liturgical."

For a book in which improvisation is central, it should be expected that some of the material appeared in earlier forms. A version of chapter 1 appeared as "Call Forwarding: Improvising the Response to the Call of Beauty," in *The Beauty of God: Theology and the Arts*, edited by Daniel J. Treier, Mark Husbands, and Roger Lundin (Downers Grove, IL: InterVarsity, 2007). Other parts of chapter 1 come from "The Fundamental Heteronomy of Jazz," *Revue*

---

6. Steve Jobs quotes Picasso, followed by the comment, "And, you know, we have always been shameless about stealing good ideas": http://www.youtube.com/watch?v=CW0DUg63lqU.http://www.youtube.com/watch?v=AxatrXaHExU.

7. This exact quote is also attributed to Franklin P. Jones (1887–1929). But doesn't this multiple attribution only provide further support for my point?

8. Pablo Picasso, *In His Words*, ed. Hiro Clark (San Francisco: Collins, 1993), 53.

internationale de philosophie 60 (2006): 453–67. Much of chapters 2 and 3 is taken from "In the Beginning, There Was Improvisation: Responding to the Call," *Verge: A Journal of Arts and Christian Faith* 1 (2011): 6–22. Portions of chapters 3 and 5 are from "Chrétien on the Call That Wounds," in *Words of Life: New Theological Turns in French Phenomenology*, edited by Bruce Ellis Benson and Norman Wirzba (New York: Fordham University Press, 2010).

Introduction

The Art of Living

The Call and Response

I think it is safe to say that there is nothing more basic to human existence than the call and response structure. It is, quite simply, the very structure of our lives.

If you've never read Scripture in terms of call and response, you may not have noticed just how frequently it occurs. It's virtually everywhere. Consider how the world comes into being: God says, "'Let there be light'; and there was light" (Gen. 1:3). So the very beginning of the world is the result of a call—God calls, and the world suddenly comes into existence.[1] The pattern does not end there: it continues in all of God's dealings with the world. God calls to Adam and Eve in the garden (his call to them *after* partaking of the fruit is particularly poignant, for now they are reluctant to respond). Then, in the midst of a broken humanity, God calls Abraham to go to a foreign land where he will make Abraham's descendants into a new nation (Gen. 12).

In Gen. 22, we get both the call and the classic form of the response. God calls out: "Abraham!" And Abraham responds: "Here

1. In chapter 3, I will revisit the issue of the creation of the world by considering a possible challenge to the *ex nihilo* account of creation.

I am" (Gen. 22:1). Abraham gives what turns out to be the standard biblical reply, saying (in Hebrew) *hinneni*. But what does *hinneni* mean? In effect, Abraham humbly says, "Here I am, your servant. I am at your disposal. Tell me what you want me to do!" This is a particularly moving passage, for God goes on to say, "Take your son, your only son Isaac, whom you love, and go to the land of Moriah, and offer him there as a burnt offering on one of the mountains that I shall show you" (Gen. 22:2). To say that Abraham must have been surprised would be a huge understatement: God is asking him to sacrifice the very son through whom God has promised to build a great nation. But Abraham does exactly what God tells him to do, and the book of Hebrews celebrates him for his faith and trust in God (Heb. 11:17).

This structure of call and response continues in Scripture. When God calls to Moses from the burning bush, God says: "Moses, Moses!" To that call, Moses replies: "Here I am" (Exod. 3:4). Similarly, God calls to Samuel who responds: "Speak, for your servant is listening" (1 Sam. 3:10). Indeed, Mary says to the angel that visits her: "Here am I, the servant of the Lord; let it be with me according to your word" (Luke 1:38). Perhaps the ultimate call in the Hebrew Bible is: "Hear, O Israel: The LORD is our God, the LORD alone" (Deut. 6:4).[2] In any case, we are constantly being called by God to give the reply "here I am," which signals our utter openness to God's command. Again, once one notes this structure, one sees it throughout all of Scripture. And it soon becomes clear that call and response is the most fundamental structure to our lives.

Consider the classic spiritual:

Hush! Hush! Somebody's calling my name
Hush! Hush! Somebody's calling my name
Hush! Hush! Somebody's calling my name
O my Lord, O my Lord, what shall I do?

Isn't this always the case? Somebody's calling my name. I hear the call and I'm faced with questions such as: What shall I do? What *shall* I do? What shall *I* do? Who is this *I* who is being called? And what happens to this *I* in being called?

2. Jean-Luc Marion claims that this is the ultimate call we receive from God. See his *Reduction and Givenness: Investigations of Husserl, Heidegger, and Phenomenology*, trans. Thomas A. Carlson (Evanston: Northwestern University Press, 1998), 196–97.

Even though this pattern of call and response goes back at least as far as creation, there is no *one* call, even in the creation narrative. Instead, there are multiple calls—calls upon calls—and thus responses upon responses, an intricate web that is ever being improvised, resulting in a ceaseless reverberation of call and response. Since this is such an important theme, we will consider it at length in chapter 1.

Presenting Ourselves as Art

In light of this most basic call—God's call to us to be at his disposal—I turn to another call, one that has to do with artistic creation. One of Saint Paul's best-known exhortations is that we present ourselves as a sacrifice to God. He writes:

> I appeal to you therefore, brothers and sisters, by the mercies of God, to present your bodies as a living sacrifice, holy and acceptable to God, which is your spiritual worship. (Rom. 12:1)

What if we were to read this verse with this small change of wording: "I appeal to you therefore, brothers and sisters, by the mercies of God, to present your bodies as a living, sacrificial *work of art*"? True, we don't usually think of ourselves as works of art. But why not? Are we not among the greatest works of art that God—the ultimate artist—has created? Without doubt, God's agency is what brings us into being; as the psalmist reminds us, "it is he that hath made us, and not we ourselves" (Ps. 100:3 KJV). However, Paul goes on in verse 2 to say, "Do not be conformed to this world, but be transformed by the renewing of your minds, so that you may discern what is the will of God—what is good and acceptable and perfect" (Rom. 12:2). People will certainly disagree as to the *extent* of God's agency in shaping us, but clearly Paul is indicating that we are very much involved in this process. That is, God has created each of us and now calls us to help shape and mold what he has created.

One way of putting this call is as follows: God has created us *in his image*. Thus, if God is a creator, we are likewise intended by God to be creators. Of course, we are not "creators" in the strong sense that God is: only God can bring forth creation from nothing. Indeed, as I argue in chapters 2 and 3, we are likely to go wrong in our thinking about ourselves as artists when we see ourselves as "like" God. But, still, we have the God-given ability to "create"—or, better yet, *improvise*—which is both a great honor and a mandate from God. Just as we are called to "be fruitful and multiply," so we are called to be creative in all that we do. After all, one of our most creative acts is precisely that of creating sons and daughters. As creators, we are called to a wonderfully meaningful life. We are not called to live in rote obedience to God; we are called to be creative in all that we do—as opposed to living a life of sheer industrial labor.

So God calls us to be artists, not in some specialized sense, but in our very being. It is *this* sense of being an artist that is most fundamental: all other senses are derivative from it. The idea that we should view ourselves as works of art becomes even clearer when we consider what Paul says in Eph. 2:10 (RSV): "For we are his workmanship, created in Christ Jesus for good works, which God prepared beforehand, that we should walk in them." The word translated as "workmanship" could quite easily—and very literally—be translated as "work of art." For the Greek term is ποίημα (*poiēma*), which happens to be a form of the term ποίησις (*poiēsis*). *Poiēsis* is used to denote the kind of knowledge involved in making art. So Paul quite explicitly says that we are God's works of art, a meaning that the English term "workmanship" fails to capture adequately. As God's artworks, we have been "created in Christ Jesus for good works," and we fulfill God's intentions for us when we "walk" in those good works. Paul reminds us that we "have been saved through faith" and that this is "the gift of God" (Eph. 2:8). Indeed, our very being is a gift!

That God has called *all of us* to be "artists" means that being an artist is *not* something just for the few, some select group of "artistically inclined," rarefied folk. Instead, the task of the artist—the great *ability* to be artists—is something given to all of us. It is a vocation to which we are all called. With that in mind, this book is directed to *everyone*. Of course, I in no way intend to denigrate those who find themselves called by God to be "artists" in the more usual and more technical sense of that word: some of us hear a definite call to be musicians, painters, poets, sculptors, or actors. Indeed, artists quite often feel truly "called" to their vocation (or avocation) as artists—and speak in these terms. In Exod. 31, God specifically tells Moses that he has called Bezalel and Oholiab to make such things as the ark of the covenant and the mercy seat. God says to Moses:

> See, I have called by name Bezalel son of Uri son of Hur, of the tribe of Judah: and I have filled him with divine spirit, with ability, intelligence, and knowledge in every kind of craft, to devise artistic designs, to work in gold, silver, and bronze, in cutting stones for setting, and in carving wood, in every kind of craft. (Exod. 31:2–5)

Talk about being called by God! Naturally, what I say here will be of *particular* interest to those who consider themselves to be "artists" in this stronger sense. But my intention is to speak to all who wish to cultivate themselves as God calls us to do. Everyone, in this most basic way, is an artist.

Perhaps this is a new way of thinking for you, though it is an old way of thinking in the Christian tradition, and even before the dawn of Christianity. The ancient Greeks saw the individual self as something like a work of art. Indeed, the word "cosmetic" goes back to the Greek verb *kosmeō* (to arrange, with positive connotations of arranging well). The idea here is that, in using cosmetics, one is more fully arranging one's body to reflect the order of the *kosmos* or universe. Of course, the Greeks sought to bring the entire self—including the mind—into an ordered whole that reflected the order of the universe. Moreover, this idea that we are all called to be artists fits with the ancient Greek conception of *mousikē*. While the principal meaning of this term that we translate as "music" or "the arts" specifically refers to tones, rhythm, dance, and words, it's much more than that. In ancient Greece, to practice *mousikē* was also to be a scholar or a philosopher. Even more broadly, it can simply mean "the cultivation of the soul." So what I am proposing is a very old idea. While this notion of seeing oneself as a work of art has more recently been picked up by such philosophers as Friedrich Nietzsche and Michel Foucault, early Christians such as Clement of Alexandria and John Chrysostom were affected by this Greek way of thinking. They realized that the cultivation of oneself requires spiritual disciplines or exercises. As Paul commends, "Examine yourselves. . . . Test yourselves" (2 Cor. 13:5). Of course, as we noted above, Paul calls us not to conform ourselves to "this world" (this *kosmos*) but to arrange ourselves according to the order to which God calls us.

A helpful way of thinking about what it could mean to be living works of art is to consider the meaning of the term "liturgy." Although "liturgy" is used almost exclusively today in connection with church services, it originally referred to how people *lived*. For instance, all of the uses of the term λειτουργία (*leitourgia*) in the New Testament describe various virtuous actions of ministry and service.[3] As Christians, our very lives should be seen as liturgical, since all that we are and do is an offering to God. J. J. von Allmen describes Jesus's own life as follows: "A superficial reading of the New Testament is sufficient to teach us that *the very life of Jesus of Nazareth is a life which is, in some sense, 'liturgical.'*" He goes on to say that the life Jesus led was "*the* life of worship."[4] By defining "liturgy" in this way, we go beyond the narrow idea that "liturgy" is merely something we do on Sunday morning or that liturgy is something only so-called liturgical churches do. True, there is something quite special about the liturgy on Sunday, and there are definitely Christian traditions that see themselves as "liturgical" in this more specialized sense. Still, human beings inevitably live in a liturgical way. James K. A. Smith has made this point quite forcefully in speaking of human beings as "*homo liturgicus.*" Working from an Augustinian framework, he argues that liturgies shape our desires and thus our lives.[5] Of course, as we will see, this is a basic insight that goes back to the early church. Liturgy was never intended to be something merely done on Sunday. Instead, liturgy is a way of life. All that we do is ultimately about worshiping God and living lives of worship.

To put this all together, we could say that the fundamental structure of our lives is that of the call and response. We are called and we respond. That call and response can rightly be considered artistic in that we are—in our being—God's works of art. That we participate with God in developing ourselves (not to mention being creators of specific artworks) is due to our call to be living works of art. And

3. The one possible exception to this is in Acts 13:2, in which the people of the church of Antioch are said to be "worshiping [λειτουργούντων] the Lord and fasting." But this reference seems to indicate only worship in general, not a particular sort of ritual.

4. J. J. von Allmen, *Worship: Its Theology and Practice* (London: Lutterworth, 1965), 21, 23.

5. James K. A. Smith, *Desiring the Kingdom: Worship, Worldview, and Cultural Formation* (Grand Rapids: Baker Academic, 2009).

the way in which we live our lives, following Jesus's example, is as liturgical beings who worship God in all that we do.

Rethinking Art

Yet here we come to an important stumbling block. For our current notion of art—particularly what we might call "high art," the kind of thing you'd find in a museum or opera house—is problematic, since it is so thoroughly infused with various "modern" or "romantic" conceptions regarding both art and artist. Yet what is so problematic about modern or romantic conceptions of the arts? One immediate problem is that central to these conceptions is the demand that art and artist be freed from the usual expectations of responsibility to the community. Further, following Immanuel Kant, we tend to envision the artist as "genius," someone who creates in an inexplicable way (think, for example, of Mozart in the film *Amadeus*). As we shall see, this way of thinking about artists and artistic creation is both harmful and largely unwarranted by actual artistic practice and therefore highly problematic. Kant was likewise influential in claiming that art does not express truth but merely emotion, and we tend to think that making art is largely about "expressing yourself." Tragically, the fact that much art has come to be seen as marginal in people's lives is the result not of the modern theory of art's having lost the day but of its having won it. For, if art communicates no truth and is merely about expressing one's feelings, then why should anyone care about it? It would seem like a frivolous luxury, which is exactly what many people think about much art. Moreover, it becomes something that is only for the *artiste*, as opposed to something for us all. *But art is too important to be sidelined as "simply" a luxury.*

What should be clear is that the modern/romantic conception of art deserves a thorough deconstruction—a thorough rethinking of its basic assumptions—which is the subject of chapter 2. Certainly the "lone creator" myth has no basis. Artists are as much dependent upon others as the rest of us, and so artistic freedom must have limits. Likewise, art involves far more than simply "expressing" oneself: artists almost inevitably communicate their vision of the world and of truth. So we must reenvision art in order to gain a sense of the communal nature of art, to reclaim art as a vehicle for truth, and to view it as something of which we are all a part.

As an antidote to the modern/romantic conception of art, I suggest the idea of improvisation, using jazz as a model.[6] By using the term "improvisation" instead of "creation," I mean to stress that artists "fabricate out of what is conveniently on hand" rather than create in the sense of "to produce where nothing was before."[7] Building upon Hans-Georg Gadamer's notion of play, I argue that improvising is inherently communal, in that we join with others and follow in the footsteps of previous improvisers. Although that communal dimension is particularly evident in "community art," all artists work within a community. A reciprocal dialogue takes place between artist and audience, which entails mutual responsibility. In place of the cult of genius, then, there is the communion of artists and audience in dialogue. Rather than unregulated freedom, there is freedom within constraints that make the play possible. Although improvisation is dependent upon a tradition that it seeks to carry on and to which it wishes to be faithful, truly faithful improvisation is never simply repetition. Further, I see our improvising as grounded in the very nature of God's creation. In creating human beings, the Triune Creator says "let us" and sets in motion a reality of continual alteration. Yet, unlike God—who creates *ex nihilo*—we create as "improvisers," *out of something*. However, if God does not simply set reality in motion but is constantly involved in that reality, then God is an "improviser" too. In *that* sense, we are improvisers in God's image.[8] What it means to be improvisers is the subject of chapter 3.

Art, Beauty, and Truth

We have already noted that, in our society, "art"—again, particularly "high art"—is viewed as an "add-on," the sort of thing one

6. My knowledge of jazz arises both from my study of it as a philosopher and from my experience as a practicing jazz musician.

7. See *Merriam-Webster's Collegiate Dictionary*, 11th ed., s.v. "improvise," and *The Oxford English Dictionary*, 2nd ed., s.v. "create."

8. Jeremy Begbie puts it as follows: "Human creativity is supremely about sharing through the Spirit in the creative purpose of the Father as he draws all things to himself through the Son." Begbie goes on to speak of our "interaction with creation" that results in both "*development*" and "*redeeming of disorder*." See his *Voicing Creation's Praise: Towards a Theology of the Arts* (Edinburgh: T&T Clark, 1991), 179.

might have once a society reaches a certain level of development and economic means. Yet this way of thinking about art is simply wrong, on at least two levels. On the one hand, there are *no* primitive cultures—no matter how "primitive" (and I am well aware just how problematic this term and such a judgment are)—that do not have some form of communal art. Art is simply ubiquitous; it's everywhere. Only if one thinks of art in the "high art" sense is it possible to think of art as being something rarefied. Rarefied art, however, is more or less an anomaly of our time compared to the millennia in which human beings have been making art. One needs only to think of those prehistoric cave paintings in France, such as in Lascaux or Chauvet (thought to be thirty-two thousand years old), to graphically demonstrate that we have long sought to express ourselves artistically. Or, to use a different sort of art, virtually all cultures have dances or other kinds of rituals of movement that have religious and communal significance. Where you find a culture or civilization, there you will undoubtedly also find art. One could put this even more strongly: precisely because you have art, therefore you have culture or civilization. Art—of various sorts—is part and parcel of our everyday experience: we find it from symphony halls to billboards, from Broadway to Hollywood, from images on the internet to iTunes.[9] As we have seen, it is very early on in God's dealings with the Israelites that he specifically calls for various artistic objects to be made according to very exacting instructions—for his glory. In other words, *our God is a God of art*. He *commands* it to be made. Moreover, he is no artistic relativist: he has highly demanding standards for what the end product should be. That God has such standards can only lead us to conclude that God must have artistic standards for us too.

God's call to Israel to make works of art according to certain standards is strongly connected with the very notion of the call. The Greek word for "call" (*kalein*) is clearly etymologically connected to the Greek word for "beauty" (*kalon*). Although we will explore this relationship in much greater depth in chapter 1, here we can note that what makes things beautiful is precisely that they call out to us. The beautiful enchants us. It makes us want to look; it makes us want to listen. Or, to go back to God's calling the

9. As should be clear here, I am using the term "art" in a very broad rather than a narrow sense.

world into being, God *first* calls and *then* pronounces it "good" (which can also be seen as God calling the world "beautiful"). In calling for art to be an intimate part of our everyday lives—even to be a way of speaking of *how* we live our lives—I mean to suggest that beauty is part of our everyday experience. That is not to suggest that there is nothing tragic or broken about the world that we experience, for we truly live in a world of brokenness and one in which even beauty itself is never fully detached from the tragic. Yet beauty is still there. Of course, I have an expansive rather than restrictive sense of the term "beautiful": there are many ways in which things can be beautiful.

More important yet, I believe that art is just as essential a way of *thinking* about the world as philosophy or physics. My intention here is to move beyond seeing art as merely about our feelings or as a way of expressing ourselves and to move toward a conception of art that is also about *truth*. Let us return to those cave paintings. Admittedly, they are very likely there to convey beauty. But do they not also say something about the lives of those who painted them? Do they, thus, not tell us something *true* about life at that time? These early artists surely were "expressing themselves," but they were doing much more than merely that. They were also making a statement about their world.

Artistic Dangers

We have already touched briefly on the problems resulting from the conceiving of art in terms of the modern/romantic paradigm. But these are not the only dangers that face us as artists. In the novel *My Name Is Asher Lev*, the character Asher Lev is warned by his mentor about becoming an "artistic whore."[10] One of the many temptations facing artists is that of providing a "pretty" view of the world (which Asher's mother keeps asking him to draw).[11] Sadly, some Christian art falls prey to this temptation. Given a world marred by sin and violence, honest art must not shy away from telling the truth. Similarly, we as works of art are always broken, even though we try so hard to act otherwise. Cornel West is helpful

10. Chaim Potok, *My Name Is Asher Lev* (New York: Anchor, 2003), 256.
11. Ibid., 17–18.

in this respect, for he reminds us of the tragic nature of our fallen world. What God has made "good" has been marred by sin. Of course, the *opposite* problem is just as dangerous. Asher's mentor warns him about "selling out" to the art world and its expectations. The artist as Christian faces both dangers, either telling lies to make us feel content or sacrificing one's identity as a Christian to fit into the "art world." To be faithful to both God and the community of believers, the artist must engage in an improvisational process of "subverting" whatever is untrue and finding ways to infiltrate and transform the world. We turn to these questions in chapter 4.

Here we come to a related though somewhat different problem. Presumably, our artworks—whether they are our drawings or our lives—should ultimately draw *us* to God. We also are called to live lives that lead *others* to God. It is instructive to consider the philosopher Jean-Luc Marion's work on icons and idols. In his highly influential text, *God without Being*, Marion reminds us that Saint Paul speaks of Jesus as the ultimate icon, the icon par excellence: "He is the image of the invisible God, the firstborn of all creation" (Col. 1:15). "Image" is the standard English translation of the Greek word εἰκών (*eikōn*). To say that Jesus is "the icon of God" is to say that Jesus both is God and, in his very being, points to God the Father. Historically, icons have been taken by the church—particularly the Eastern church, though not it alone—to be images that lead us to God. As such, they are like windows that do not draw attention to themselves but act as portals to God. As an example, we might say that a good sermon should not leave us thinking "what a wonderful preacher!" but "what a wonderful God!" The preacher is merely an icon. In contrast, Marion likens idols to *mirrors*, for they allow us only to see ourselves: "The idol depends on the gaze that it satisfies, since if the gaze did not desire to satisfy itself in the idol, the idol would have no dignity for it."[12] We value idols precisely because they allow us to gaze upon ourselves.

We are called to be icons, not idols. Our lives—as works of art—should point both ourselves and others to God. Such a goal raises two very closely connected questions. On the one hand, to what extent are the art that we create and the lives that we live designed for us and our pleasures, versus for God and his pleasure? Perhaps

---

12. Jean-Luc Marion, *God without Being*, trans. Thomas A. Carlson (Chicago: University of Chicago Press, 1991), 10.

there is ultimately no problem here, since the answer might simply be "both." Yet, often art is seen as something one does merely for oneself, a point that we consider in chapters 2 and 4. On the other hand, there is clearly an artistic difficulty in providing a glimpse of God that is paralleled by the theological difficulty of writing about God. Marion reminds us that no image of God (literal or figurative) is "adequate" to God, who is a "saturated phenomenon" in the sense that God's fullness exceeds our grasp. Yet we are still called to tell the narrative of God's redemptive work in history and become partakers with God through art, providing ways of seeing and hearing that speak to new generations of both believers and unbelievers. Part of the artistic work is to "deconstruct" images of God that are inadequate or inaccurate, and art is a powerful medium for challenging the ways in which we conceive God. Yet another part of our artistic responsibility is to become icons ourselves. In other words, as we improvisationally compose our lives, we can become icons that point to God.

Liturgy of the Word and Eucharist

So far, our emphasis here has been on liturgy as a way of life. It is something we do every day as part of our very being. Such is exactly the emphasis one finds in *Liturgy for Living*, in which the authors make an important distinction: The term "intensive liturgy" describes "what happens when Christians assemble to worship God." "Extensive liturgy" describes "what happens when Christians leave the assembly to conduct their daily affairs." As the authors go on to say, "the two [types of liturgy] are mutually dependent."[13] Although we can quite rightly be described as *living* liturgically, there is of course liturgy that takes the form of "worship services." All churches have their liturgies—their ways of organizing themselves, their specific rites and rituals. Yet even those churches that closely follow a "script" (e.g., written instructions or something like *The Book of Common Prayer*) are always improvising, for liturgy is an event that happens anew each time it is incarnated. Using the Greek notion of καιρός [*kairos*], Hans-Georg Gadamer speaks of

---

13. Charles P. Price and Louis Weil, *Liturgy for Living* (New York: Seabury, 1979), 296.

"festival time," in which something is repeated in such a way that there is both repetition and development.[14] Consider a festival that recurs each year: each time that it occurs, it does so anew. In festival time, we are taken out of the ordinary sense of time in which minute follows minute; we are moved into a different sense of time. Each time we worship, we celebrate the life, death, and resurrection of Christ and his victory over sin and death. And, in that moment, clock time takes a back seat to festival time. Yet liturgy is (to cite the literal meaning of the term) truly "work,"[15] for it requires that we work hard to "hear" God's voice and to move into a posture of worship. To say that worship is improvisational means that we must be constantly seeking new ways of declaring God's glory and new ways of hearing God's voice.

The very structure of the liturgy of the Word and Eucharist is constituted by the call and response. We are always already called to proclaim the Word, and the Word calls out to all assembled. In turn, we respond to the call and yet also turn outward to call to both those in the assembly and those outside of it. Of course, as Jean-Louis Chrétien points out, the call is only truly heard *in the response*. So the call cannot be thought without the response. Similarly, the Eucharist is enacted both because Jesus has called us to "do this in remembrance" and because we are (to use a term from Marion) "the gifted."[16] That is, we have been given not just the gift of salvation but also the gift of the identity of being Christ's body. In turn, we offer to God not merely our souls and bodies but also our gifts of bread and wine. The call and response structure is mirrored in our receiving and giving back to God.

14. Hans-Georg Gadamer, *The Relevance of the Beautiful and Other Essays*, trans. Nicholas Walker, ed. Robert Bernasconi (Cambridge: Cambridge University Press, 1986), 39–42.

15. The Greek word for liturgy literally means "the work of the people." We will return to this definition in chapter 5.

16. The word translated as "the gifted" is the French term *l'adonné*. Literally, this means "the devoted" or even "the addicted." Despite this difficulty, "the gifted" gets at the important aspect of reception. See Jean-Luc Marion, *Being Given: Toward a Phenomenology of Givenness*, trans. Jeffrey L. Kosky (Stanford: Stanford University Press, 2002), 268.

1

The Call and the Response

Heeding the Call

Upon waiting for the service to begin at Saint Sabina's on the south side of Chicago, I was pleased to hear a lovely buzz of warm fellowship. Suddenly, a voice boomed out: "I was glad when they said, 'Let us go into the house of the Lord.'" A hush fell over the congregation, though there were scattered responses of "Amen" and "Praise the Lord." To put all of this in context, I should mention that the service was on the Sunday after the Friday night on which three children were shot just outside the church. Not surprisingly, virtually the entire service was connected in some way with that event. Cameras from all the local television networks were there. And everyone was waiting to hear what the rather controversial Father Michael Pfleger was going to say.

When Father Pfleger pointed out that it is when we are being particularly effective as Christ's followers that the devil is most likely to "come for us," there were shouts of affirmation. The church had recently started Friday night events designed precisely to keep children from the parish off the street and thus safe. So the shootings were particularly disturbing. Father Pfleger called for all of the children to come forward and stand around the altar. A prayer for protection was said for them. Then, each child was asked to turn to another, make the sign of the cross on the other

33

child's forehead, and say, "I cover you with his blood." Toward the
end of the service, all of the men were asked to come forward and
were led to chant "It's On"—that is, the fight against the powers
of evil was "on," and the parish was being called upon to take
part. The continued response was the sign of willingness to take
on this weighty responsibility.

As is typical of African American worship, the entire service
had the structure of call and response. Consider simply the things
that I mentioned in the paragraph above: the call to worship, the
children coming forward and marking one another with the sign
of the cross, and the men chanting, "It's On." Although Pfleger is
white, he has thoroughly absorbed the rhythm and style of black
preaching. For instance, at one point he said, "Somebody shout
out, 'This is our time.'" And he expected a vigorous response. Of
course, there were constant responses to what he had to say, as well
as continuous calls that demanded responses. But it was one of the
songs that particularly exemplified this call and response structure,
titled "Here I Am to Worship": "Here I am to worship, here I am
to bow down, here I am to say that you're my God." It is this "here
I am" that is important.

In the introduction, we noted that the call and response structure
is basic to human existence. We also saw that the very *nature* of
the call constitutes the warp and woof of Scripture. We noted that
the world comes into existence by way of God's call. But the pattern does not end there: it continues on into all of God's dealings
with the world, whether it is God calling to Adam and Eve in the
garden or calling to Abraham to go to a foreign land or calling to
Moses from a burning bush. We are constantly being called by God
to give the reply *hinneni*—here I am, at your disposal, waiting for
your command. The call calls out for a response.

African American spirituals are particularly illustrative of the call
and response structure of improvisation. Spirituals such as "Hush!
Somebody's Calling My Name" speak of a call that demands a
response. Both artist and audience need to see themselves as involved in this call and response. Worship is one way this call and
response is played out, and artistic improvising is also inherently a
"call" to an audience that seeks for a "response." Artistically, our
response is that we become improvisers with God and with each
other. Yet the response is often not just back to God but also out to
others. We are called and, in turn, we call out to others. Unlike the

modern conception of the artwork as "finished," improvisational art is constantly open to being performed anew. Because artistic improvisation is a continual development of what we have been given, there is a sense in which it constantly grows and moves beyond itself. Or, put differently, *we grow and move beyond ourselves as constantly improvised works of art.*

In what follows, we will examine what I take to be reflections of God's beauty in creation. If all beauty originates from God, then all beauty found in the world is a reflected beauty. Rather than attempting to define beauty, to provide the "essence" of beauty, or even to reflect on beautiful things per se, I will consider beauty by way of the call. Here we will be following the call of Jean-Louis Chrétien as laid out in his book *The Call and the Response.*[1] There Chrétien reminds us of just how central this structure of call and response is to creaturely existence, and how intimately connected to goodness and beauty it is. Then we will unpack Chrétien's analysis of the call, likewise turning to Hans Urs von Balthasar. Finally, we will consider how we might work out the call and response in black spirituals and jazz, and then reflect upon how they likewise provide an example of beauty.

It is, I think, appropriate to consider music that originates from the margins, from those oppressed and considered the least. For Jesus—whom Paul terms the "icon" of God (see 2 Cor. 4:4)—self identifies with the hungry, the thirsty, the stranger, the naked, and the prisoner, saying, "Just as you did it to one of the least of these who are members of my family, you did it to me" (Matt. 25:40). The beauty that is reflected by the marginalized is a broken beauty, one that reflects a God who not only takes a stand with the oppressed and broken but also becomes oppressed and broken himself. And yet that broken beauty likewise points to the eschatological beauty of the risen, reigning Lord.

Beauty as the Call

There is absolutely no sense of "beauty for beauty's sake" in Chrétien: as he says, "things and forms do not beckon us because they

1. Jean-Louis Chrétien, *The Call and the Response*, trans. Anne A. Davenport (New York: Fordham University Press, 2004).

are beautiful in themselves, *for their own sake*, as it were. Rather, we call them beautiful precisely because they call us and recall us."[2] Here we have a surprising reversal. Chrétien is clear regarding the relation of call, beauty, and goodness. But it is the *order* of them that he puts into question. "Beautiful, *kalon*, is what comes from a call, *kalein*," he says.[3] So the call is what constitutes the beautiful, rather than the other way around. Things are beautiful precisely because they call out to us. Or we might put this the other way around: God's call precedes the pronouncement of beauty. "Let there be light," says God, and only *after* calling it into being does he then reflect on its goodness (Gen. 1:3–4). In this sense, *kaleō* (to call) is more primordial than *kalon*. As Chrétien puts it, "The word 'beautiful' is not primary, but responds and corresponds to the first call, which is the call sent by thought construed as a power to call and to name."[4]

Yet the creation of light lacks the dimension of a *human* call. Light may "respond" by illuminating, but a person called by God responds by both a readiness to hear and a readiness to act. What takes place in the human call and response is a crucial reversal. Emmanuel Levinas puts it as follows: "Here I am (*me voici*)! The accusative here is remarkable: here I am, under your eyes, at your service, your obedient servant."[5] In other words, the subject is now truly *subject* to the other, the one who calls, and so stands in the accusative case. Similarly, Balthasar, influenced by the famed writer on acting Konstantin Stanislavsky, speaks of a *disponibilité* in which "the whole human system is made available."[6] In being called, we are at the other's disposal.[7]

2. Ibid., 3 (italics added).
3. Ibid., 7.
4. Ibid.
5. Emmanuel Levinas, "God and Philosophy," in *Basic Philosophical Writings*, ed. Adriaan T. Peperzak, Simon Critchley, and Robert Bernasconi (Bloomington: Indiana University Press, 1996), 146.
6. Hans Urs von Balthasar, *Theo-Drama: Theological Dramatic Theory*, vol. 1, *Prolegomena*, trans. Graham Harrison (San Francisco: Ignatius, 1988), 288. Here Balthasar references Konstantin Stanislavsky, *Das Geheimnis des schauspielerischen Erfolges* (Zurich: Scientia, n.d.), 168.
7. Of course, this raises a question: What if the call of the *human* other is unreasonable? I turn to these kinds of questions (specifically, the question of our responsibility to others) in chapter 4. I address the issue of ethical responsibility in *Graven Ideologies: Nietzsche, Derrida, and Marion on Modern Idolatry* (Downers Grove,

Yet how does beauty call, and what is its attraction? While the Hebraic priority of the voice has often been contrasted with the Hellenic priority of sight, the "call" can come in either form, or another form altogether. Relating his enlightenment from Diotima in the *Symposium*, Socrates speaks of moving from an *eros* for the body to an *eros* for the soul to an *eros* for beauty itself.[8] Ultimately, this *eros* for—or, we might well say, call to—beauty is disconnected from both sight and sound. So it would seem that the call may be delivered through sight or sound, or even something else. However, Chrétien points out that, even in the Socratic dialogue *Symposium*, "vision, at every step, produces speech in response [e.g., the very speech that Socrates is making at the banquet]" and so concludes that "visible beauty calls for spoken beauty."[9] What exactly, though, is beauty's allure? In commenting on Plato, the neo-Platonist philosopher Proclus makes the insightful etymological observation that beauty calls "because it enchants and charms [*kalein*]."[10] Chrétien concludes that the charm beauty exerts results in "voice, speech, and music."[11] Of course, Chrétien is overstating the case. No doubt beauty *often* results in speech and music, but it can likewise move us to paint or sculpt (though one can also see these as "giving voice" to a kind of speech).

Yet Proclus does more than define beauty in terms of enchantment and charm, for he likewise connects this enchantment with God. In his *Platonic Theology*, he writes, "Beauty converts all things to itself, sets them in motion, causes them to be possessed by the divine, and *recalls them to itself through the intermediary of love.*"[12] We find this same connection between beauty and God in Dionysius—or Pseudo-Dionysius—again by way of the call: "Beauty 'calls' all

IL: InterVarsity Press, 2002). Here I follow Levinas's custom of capitalizing the word "Other." For Levinas, the Other can be both the human and the divine Other, and such is the case here.

8. *Symposium* 210a–e, in Plato, *The Collected Dialogues*, ed. Edith Hamilton and Huntington Cairns (Princeton: Princeton University Press, 1961). Further citations of Plato will be from this edition.

9. Chrétien, *Call and the Response*, 11.

10. Proclus, *Sur le premier Alcibiade de Platon*, ed. and trans. A. Segonds (Paris: Belles Lettres, 1986), 2:361 (cited in ibid., 12).

11. Chrétien, *Call and the Response*, 12.

12. Proclus, *The Platonic Theology*, trans. Thomas Taylor (El Paso: Selene, 1988), 77. Here I am following the quote as translated by Anne A. Davenport in Chrétien, *Call and the Response*, 9–10 (italics added).

things to itself (whence it is called 'beauty'),'' writes Dionysius, who makes it clear that "Beauty" here is another name for God (in his text titled *The Divine Names*).[13]

So beauty enchants and this enchantment comes from God. But, once moved, how do we forward the call on to others? The answer to that question can best be found in analyzing the initial call itself. And here I turn to Balthasar. For, although the language of call and response is not central to Balthasar's thought to the degree that it is in Chrétien, his description of how beauty charms us is remarkably in line with Chrétien. Yet Balthasar adds at least three elements that help clarify the call. All three of these elements can be found in the following passage from the *Theological Aesthetics*:

> The form as it appears to us is beautiful only because the delight that it arouses in us is founded upon the fact that, in it, the truth and goodness of the depths of reality itself are manifested and bestowed, and this manifestation and bestowal reveal themselves to us as being something infinitely and inexhaustibly valuable and fascinating.[14]

Let me enumerate these elements. First, whereas secular liberalism/modernism (particularly as exemplified by Immanuel Kant) disconnects the traditional transcendentals of the good, the true, and the beautiful, Balthasar reconnects them and makes them truly part of the created order.[15] Classically, of course, the ancient Greeks took the good, the true, and the beautiful to be very closely interconnected. That is, whatever is good is also beautiful, and whatever is beautiful is true. Further, for the Greeks, speaking of something as being beautiful is not simply a way of describing one's own feelings but actually identifies a characteristic in the object itself.

13. Pseudo-Dionysius, *The Divine Names* 701c–d, in *The Complete Works*, trans. Colin Luibheid and Paul Rorem (New York: Paulist, 1987). The English translation uses "bids" in place of "calls." But, since the verb is *kaloun* in the Greek text, "calls" seems a more accurate translation.

14. Hans Urs von Balthasar, *The Glory of the Lord: A Theological Aesthetics*, vol. 1, *Seeing the Form* (San Francisco: Ignatius; New York: Crossroad, 1983), 118.

15. Here I am indebted to Oliver Davies's piece "The Theological Aesthetics," in *The Cambridge Companion to Hans Urs von Balthasar*, ed. Edward T. Oakes, SJ, and David Moss (Cambridge: Cambridge University Press, 2004), 131–42.

Balthasar revives both this connection and the belief that goodness, truth, and beauty really *exist*. Second, and closely related,
in Balthasar "the beauty of the world" and "theological beauty"
are once again connected, as they were in Thomas Aquinas.[16] This
reconnection is why Balthasar insists that his is a "theological
aesthetics" rather than an "aesthetic theology." This means that
God's call to us is very much connected to the beauty of the earth,
even while surpassing and pointing beyond that earthly beauty.
Third, the possibility of the call is due to what Balthasar calls a
"double and reciprocal *ekstasis* [going out of oneself]—God's
'venturing forth' to man and man's to God."[17] Balthasar goes so
far as to speak of the "elevation of man to participate in [God's]
glory."[18]

In both Chrétien's and Balthasar's accounts of the call, then,
participation is central. But how do we participate in the call? In one
sense, that participation is possible because God both transcends the
world and yet is reflected by it. One can—on this point—agree with
the theologian John Milbank, who writes that "participation can
be extended also to language, history and culture: the whole realm
of human *making*" precisely because "human making participates
in a God who is infinite poetic utterance."[19] While it seems to me
that Milbank here unduly limits participation to *poiēsis* (which, as
we have seen, is the ancient Greek term for artistic making)—and
I would want to broaden it to include *phronēsis* (i.e., the ancient
Greek term for practical wisdom, knowing how to act in practical
situations)—the context for these reflections certainly makes *poiēsis*
an appropriate way in which to participate in the divine beauty. Of
course, there are different ways to think of *poiēsis*. The notion of
artistic "creation" has been a guiding one in the arts. As we noted
in the introduction, "creation" tends to carry certain problematic
overtones. Given that the call always precedes us—and is what makes
it possible for us to call in response—I have suggested replacing
it with "improvisation" (a suggestion I develop at greater length
in chapter 3). Here I will develop that notion in terms of black
spirituals and jazz.

16. Balthasar, *Glory of the Lord*, 1:80.
17. Ibid., 1:126.
18. Ibid., 1:125.
19. John Milbank, *Being Reconciled: Ontology and Pardon* (London: Routledge,
2003), ix.

Improvising the Response

Black spirituals and jazz illuminate well what takes place in the call and response. At least two things are worth noting: (1) the call always *precedes* me, and (2) the improvised response is always a repetition and an improvisation.

The first point, then, is that the call always precedes me. It is not just that the response is a response to a prior call; it is that even the call in these songs echoes yet a prior call. That call can be spelled out in terms of the previous performance of these pieces. But it can likewise be traced back to earlier calls. For these songs are, in effect, echoes of echoes—going back to the call from God at the beginning of the world. Or, in the case of spirituals, to Jesus's call to his disciples. Jesus says to Peter and Andrew, "Follow me, and I will make you fish for people" (Matt. 4:19). That call is, in turn, broadened by the Great Commission, in which the disciples—and, by extension, *we*—are called to "go therefore and make disciples of all nations." Here we become explicit messengers of God's call to the world. We do not call in our name, but "in the name of the Father and of the Son and of the Holy Spirit" (Matt. 28:19). This is why Chrétien speaks of it being "always too late already for there to be an origin,"[20] for the origin of the present call far precedes it. Thus, the responding is both to a present call—one here and now—and to the calls that have preceded it. Scripture echoes this kind of echoing of calls: so, for example, when Jesus calls for repentance, he is echoing God's multiple calls to Israel through Moses and the prophets.

To improvise in jazz, then, is to respond to a call, to join in something that is always already in progress. One becomes an improviser by becoming part of the discourse of jazz. While it would take considerably deeper analysis than we have time for here to explain what is involved in becoming a jazz musician and learning how to improvise, we can briefly summarize what happens as follows. Speaking with Pierre Bourdieu, we might say that one must cultivate a *habitus*—a way of being that is both nurtured by and results in what Bourdieu terms "regulated improvisations."[21] They

---

20. Chrétien, *Call and the Response*, 5.
21. Pierre Bourdieu, *Outline of a Theory of Practice*, trans. Richard Nice (Cambridge: Cambridge University Press, 1977), 78.

are "regulated" precisely by the constraints that make jazz "jazz" and not something else. Of course, we could also use the term "liturgy" in place of *habitus*, for becoming a jazz musician is becoming a part of the institution of jazz, which exists as a regulative practice that shapes and forms us.[22] The liturgy of jazz is particularly dependent on *listening*, and learning to listen is the precondition for all future improvisation—especially when one improvises with others. So we can say that each improvisation is like a response to improvisations of the past. To become an improviser, one must have an intimate knowledge of past improvisations and the possible conditions for those improvisations (i.e., the conventions of improvising). To be able to improvise means one is steeped in a particular tradition (whether jazz or the blues or Baroque music) and knows how to respond to the call of other improvisers. Although we tend to think of jazz improvisation in terms of spontaneity, that quality of improvisation—while undoubtedly present—is often greatly exaggerated. It is also remarkably paradoxical. Not only are many "improvisations" often significantly "scripted," but spontaneity is only possible when one is well prepared. Contrary to what many believe about jazz, a jazz musician doesn't just get up on stage and start blowing notes. It takes a great deal of work to be spontaneous. It also takes a significant knowledge of improvisations of the past, for they provide the guidelines for improvisations of the present and future. Consider what the trumpeter Wynton Marsalis says in response to a question of how he achieved his remarkable level of success:

> I would listen to records, I would buy all these etude books. Any money I would make on little pop gigs I would buy trumpets or books with it. I would get all the etude books, I would go to different teachers, I would call people, and really seek the knowledge. I would go to music camp in the summer time. Practice, listen to the recordings of Adolph Herseth [the principal trumpet in the Chicago Symphony Orchestra for many years], or Clifford Brown, trying to learn the records.[23]

22. Alasdair MacIntyre speaks of a practice as a social activity regulated by goals and standards. Practices are themselves embedded in wider traditions that make sense of those practices. See Alasdair MacIntyre, *After Virtue*, 2nd ed. (Notre Dame, IN: University of Notre Dame Press, 1981), 190.

23. "Music's Jazz Maestro," an online interview with Wynton Marsalis, January 8, 1991. See http://www.achievement.org/autodoc/page/mar0int-4.

Further, "being spontaneous" is not something one simply wills. Keith Johnstone notes that it is the "decision not to try and control the future" that allows for spontaneity.[24] Although Johnstone is speaking of theater, his point is just as valid for improvisation as a whole. The implication here is that one opens oneself up to the future to allow something to happen. But, of course, that opening oneself up to the future is only possible by being fully prepared, and that requires a thorough grounding in the tradition. In jazz, knowing the past is what makes the future possible. In the same way, learning to be a *Christian* improviser, one must know the entire context: Scripture and the ways in which Scripture has been interpreted in the past. In short, one must be part of a *community* of improvisers.

Of course, in realizing the debt to and dependency upon the past, the jazz musician is aware that any response to the call is made possible by a *gift*. The call is a gift to me, something that comes—like life itself—ultimately unbidden and simply disseminated. Former Archbishop of Canterbury Rowan Williams reminds us that art "always approaches the condition of being both recognition and transmission of gift, gratuity or excess."[25] There is, of course, a long tradition (both inside and outside the Christian tradition) in which the ability to paint or sculpt or improvise has been seen as a gift, something simply bestowed upon one that calls for responsibility on the part of the receiver to cultivate, nurture, and exercise.[26] In this sense, both the ability and the products that arise from that ability are gifts. And such gifts are hardly given simply to Christians or to the religious faithful. Indeed, not only are these gifts regularly given to those who aren't Christians, they are sometimes—perhaps often—given to people who neither appreciate them nor are thankful for them, and may not exercise them well or even at all. In the introduction, we noted that Scripture speaks of artists as

24. Keith Johnstone, *Impro: Improvisation and the Theatre* (New York: Theatre Arts Books, 1979), 32.

25. Rowan Williams, *Grace and Necessity: Reflections on Art and Love* (Harrisburg, PA: Morehouse, 2005), 163.

26. Just as an example, I note that at the Iridium Jazz Club (New York) website one finds the following regarding the famed jazz guitarist Les Paul: "Les Paul says his greatest God-given gifts are perfect pitch, a love for music with the ability to learn it quickly, and the curiosity and persistence of an inventor who wants to know 'how things tick'" (http://www.iridiumjazzclub.com/les.shtml).

having been specially called by God. In Exod. 31, God handpicks Bezalel and Oholiab to serve as artists to design the tabernacle, in effect a large tent that could be erected and then dismantled to move to another place. Bezalel's name means "the shadow of God" and Oholiab's name means "my tent is the Father-God."[27] Yet God does not simply anoint them as artists: he likewise gives painstaking details as to exactly how he wishes the tabernacle to be constructed. In other words, God clearly has an idea of what is meet and right, as well as what would make the tabernacle a thing of beauty. As Frank E. Gaebelein puts it: "Think of it! The Lord himself the divine patron of the arts!"[28] Yet, if one takes that gift character seriously, then one senses a kind of responsibility for exercising artistic gifts. Although it is the theatrical rather than the jazz improvisers who speak in these terms, the call is like an "offer" that can be either "accepted" or "blocked."[29] To "accept" the call is to respond in kind, to say "yes" to what is being offered and thus develop the call in order simultaneously to send it back and send it forward. And that is exactly what Bezalel and Oholiab do: they respond to God and they present an offering to the people of Israel.

Second, my response is never mine alone. To be sure, I speak for myself, but I also speak for others and in their name. Even my identity as an improviser is interconnected with those of other improvisers. I may still have an identity, but it is hardly fixed or simple.

This question of identity naturally leads to my third point, which is that my response is always both a repetition and an innovation. Chrétien writes of the strange logic of improvisation (even though he is hardly thinking explicitly of improvisation, let alone jazz): "Our response can only repeat. It starts by repeating. Yet it does not repeat by restating."[30] He goes on to explain this enigmatic

27. R. Alan Cole, *Exodus: An Introduction and Commentary* (Leicester, UK: Inter-Varsity, 1973), 210.

28. Frank E. Gaebelein, *The Christian, the Arts, and Truth: Regaining the Vision of Greatness*, ed. D. Bruce Lockerbie (Portland, OR: Multnomah, 1985), 64. Gaebelein also muses on the fact that Bezalel's name is particularly appropriate for his calling as a "godly artist and craftsman."

29. "I call anything that an actor does an 'offer'. Each offer can either be accepted, or blocked. . . . A block is anything that prevents the action from developing" (Johnstone, *Impro*, 97).

30. Ibid., 25.

claim by saying that there is a kind of space that is opened up *in ourselves* that gives us a voice so that we can pass on the call without mere repetition. We hear the call and we translate it into an idiom of our own. Yet how should we think of this mélange of sameness and difference, a repetition that is not merely a repetition but also a development?

A particularly influential way of thinking about this identity and difference is Henry Louis Gates Jr.'s notion of "signifyin(g)."[31] It is interesting—and quite instructive for my point here—that Gates admits that he is in effect improvising on Jacques Derrida's notion of *différance*.[32] Gates says that "all texts Signify upon other texts," but we could modify that by simply saying that "all improvisations improvise upon other improvisations."[33] On Gates's view, there are two ways that one "signifies." Given that Gates is providing an account of how Africans and African Americans relate to white culture, one of those ways of "signifyin(g)" is repetition with "a compelling sense of difference based on the black vernacular."[34] Yet signifyin(g) can also take the form of "homage," in which one performs the music of another—or improvises upon the improvisations of another—as (and here I quote Gates) "a gesture of admiration and respect."[35] John P. Murphy provides a fine example of that homage by analyzing a solo of Joe Henderson's that utilizes a theme from Charlie Parker's improvisation on "Buzzy."

> It is the "Buzzy" theme that tenor-saxophonist Joe Henderson chooses to transform during his improvisations on two performances of a 12-bar blues in F. The first transformation is heard on his "If". . . . One might argue that the appearance of Parker's motive at the end of Henderson's third chorus is a coincidence, but the fact that Henderson moves on to construct the entire next

31. Henry Louis Gates Jr., *The Signifying Monkey: A Theory of African-American Literary Criticism* (New York: Oxford University Press, 1988), 46. Here I simply assume that "signifyin(g)" can have a positive function, though I discuss this question in detail in my article "The Fundamental Heteronomy of Jazz," *Revue internationale de philosophie* 60 (2006): 453–67.

32. For more on the notion of *différance*, see Jacques Derrida, "*Différance*," in *Margins of Philosophy*, trans. Alan Bass (Chicago: University of Chicago Press, 1982), 3–27.

33. Gates, *Signifying Monkey*, xxiv.

34. Ibid., xxii.

35. Ibid., xxvii and 63.

chorus on a restatement of the motive in its original form, followed by two transformations, shows it to be a conscious manipulation of Parker's idea.[36]

Here we have a blend of repetition and transformation, but one that is clearly designed to pay a kind of homage to Charlie Parker. Or, to take a different example, Paul Berliner provides a fascinating genealogy of a particular jazz lick from 1946 to 1992. It starts with Billy Eckstine and Miles Davis and makes its way through Bud Powell, Clifford Brown, Dave Young, Paul Chambers, Red Garland, Ella Fitzgerald, Cannonball Adderly, The Manhattan Transfer, John Scofield, Benny Green, and Christian McBride.[37]

Anyone familiar with jazz realizes that these names cover a rather long and wide sweep in the life of jazz: different styles, different time periods, different generations. So a given lick can constantly be transformed improvisationally and yet have enough "sameness" to have a continued identity. Yet each of these voices adds something along the way. An example like this provides us with a way of conceptualizing differing voices all improvising in their own respective ways upon the same basic line. And this, in turn, helps us think about how the call of beauty can go forth in so many different ways and be continually transformed.

Beauty and the Call to Live Artistically

It may seem that in the previous section we left beauty in order to focus on improvisation. Yet beauty has been present all along. Since beauty *is* precisely the call and its enchantment, beauty is part of improvisation. Here we need to link beauty, the call, and improvisation for the practicing artist.

If we can rightly say that our artistic creation is a participation in God's making or *poiēsis* (which I believe we can), then our calls are rightly seen as a continuation of God's calls. Of course, the beautiful is to be taken as a transcendental that is connected to goodness and truth. With that in mind, all art that reflects beauty, goodness,

---

36. John P. Murphy, "Jazz Improvisation: The Joy of Influence," *Black Perspective in Music* 18, no. 1/2 (1990): 10.

37. Paul Berliner, *Thinking in Jazz: The Infinite Art of Improvisation* (Chicago: University of Chicago Press, 1994), 576–78.

and truth is beautiful, good, and true. Of course, this connection of beauty with goodness and truth does not simplify the situation but instead adds complexity, as we will see in the following chapter.

We receive God's call and improvise a response that goes back to God and forward to all of creation. It is indeed incumbent upon us—in light of the Great Commission—to spread that call. And art—whether aural or visual—is a powerful way of carrying forth God's call. Here again we must connect *poiēsis* to *phronēsis* for two reasons. First, the art we make is in effect a response to God's call and so it ought to be directed toward *phronēsis*—our practical ability to act in the world.[38] Making art is not some *other* thing that is somehow disconnected from life itself. Rather, art making *flows from* living our lives and likewise influences our lives in deep and profound ways. There is a poem by Rainer Maria Rilke titled "The Archaic Torso of Apollo" that ends with the memorable line "You must change your life." What is so remarkable about the poem is that an arresting description of this torso of Apollo is what brings about this revelation. Yet this shows that art—even something like a statue—has the power to affect us *so that we live differently.* Second, and even more important than the first point, if we are called to live artistically, we must cultivate a certain *kind of being.* Liturgy is our way of life. We noted in the introduction that Paul exhorts us to present ourselves as living sacrifices in Rom. 12, and speaks of us as God's *poiēma* in Eph. 2:10. As we also considered, while we are the result of God's handiwork, Paul makes it clear in Rom. 1:2 that we are to be "transformed by the renewing of [our] minds." So, while God *creates* us, he invites us to have a hand in how we develop.

Although we will turn at length in chapter 5 to the way the church has historically considered its members as living works of art (and has linked the notion of personal and corporate liturgy), here we can note that early on in Christian theology we indeed find the idea that we should consider ourselves to be works of art. For instance, the church father John Chrysostom encourages those wishing to follow the way of Christian faith to consider their souls to be like paintings or pieces of sculpture. Specifically, he makes an analogy

---

38. *Phronēsis* is a Greek word that describes our most common experiences of *acting* in the world. How to brush your teeth, how to drive a car, how be a moral person—these are all examples of *phronēsis*. *Poēsis* is the Greek term for "making" a finished product.

between the painter drawing a preliminary sketch and one's development as a Christian. The painter works with the preliminary drawing to alter and shape it in the same way that Christians alter and shape their ways of being. He likewise draws an analogy between Christian parents rearing their children and painters and sculptors:

> To each of you fathers and mothers I say, just as we see artists fashioning their paintings and statues with great precision, so we must care for these wondrous statues of ours. Painters when they have set the canvas on the easel paint on it day by day to accomplish their purpose. Sculptors, too, working in marble, proceed in a similar manner; they remove what is superfluous and add what is lacking. Even so you must proceed. Like the creators of statues do you give all your leisure to fashioning these wondrous statues for God.[39]

We are the artworks that God has created, though God gives us the great honor of further fashioning ourselves. Of course, we do not do so all by ourselves; indeed, Chrysostom here exhorts parents to be part of the process with their children. By extension, so all of us, as part of the Christian community, participate in fashioning one another to become beautiful works of art. This process is a lifelong quest—a continual movement toward beauty. And such is our calling.

Yet, if we are truly artists, we must address some fundamental questions on the nature of art and artistic creation. That is the subject of the next chapter.

39. John Chrysostom, *Address on Vainglory and the Right Way for Parents to Bring up Their Children*, in M. L. Laistner, *Christianity and Pagan Culture in the Later Roman Empire* (Ithaca, NY: Cornell University Press, 1951), 22. John Chrysostom, *De inani gloria* 22 (Sources chrétiennes 188:106–8).

2

Deconstructing
the Discourse of Art

"You are entering a religion called painting. . . . Its values are goyish and pagan. Its concepts are goyish and pagan. Its way of life is goyish and pagan. . . . Think carefully of what you are doing before you make your decision."[1] Those are the stern words of warning that Jacob Kahn gives his pupil Asher Lev, a young Hasidic Jew who aspires to be a painter—something to which Hasidic Jews aren't supposed to aspire. The story of Asher Lev can be read as a violent clash between two "religions"—Asher's Judaism and art.

Somewhat similarly, my former colleague Alva Steffler speaks of Christian artists experiencing not just "alienation as artists" but also "the seeming ambivalence of their church."[2] No doubt, Christians have often been suspicious of artists both outside and within their midst: What are artists up to? Why do they say things in such complicated ways (and why can't they just say them more simply)? But there is a further problem that Steffler alludes to with the word "ambivalence": Christians have often wondered about the

1. Chaim Potok, *My Name Is Asher Lev* (New York: Anchor, 2003), 213.
2. Alva Steffler, "Chronology of a Movement," in *Faith + Vision: Twenty-Five Years of Christians in the Visual Arts*, ed. Cameron J. Anderson and Sandra Bowden (Baltimore: Square Halo, 2005), 147.

value of art. While art that can be sung in church or used in Sunday school has a very obvious purpose, much art seems to have very little purpose, or none at all. To put this another way, in a world in which there is hunger and suffering, isn't it simply too frivolous to create art? Shouldn't artists be doing something that is more valuable to society? These kinds of concerns are well illustrated by the experience of one of Wheaton College's former art students, Emily Cottrill, who says, "God made me to be an artist. He gave me that talent. He made me to be able to get excited about certain things. That's my response to God, to his world, to his message of salvation. When you see something that's so wonderful, you want to join in." But not all of her fellow students saw it that way. As the writer of the article that featured her comments went on to say, "by the end of her sophomore year, she was sick of her peers' indifference to her calling. She was fed up with comments that suggested that art is a waste of time, a field for slackers and weirdos." In her journal, Emily had written: "I felt I had to justify myself. Not to the world, but to me. That is a terrible thing. I am a child of God. God made me a person who sees the world in a manner that is different from most perceptions. He gave me the urge to create."[3]

Yet this raises the basic question of what it means to be an artist. As it turns out, we in the twenty-first century think largely in terms inherited from the late eighteenth and early nineteenth centuries. In other words, our conceptions about art are deeply *modern*. So, before we can speak positively about what it means to be living works of art, we need to consider our current conceptions about art and artists. Practically, we need a kind of "deconstruction" (a taking apart and putting into question) of the dominant way of thinking about art and artists before we can begin to rebuild by putting a new vision of artistic endeavor in place.

The "Modern" or "Romantic" Discourse of Art

What exactly makes a clash virtually inevitable not just for Asher Lev but also for artists who are Christian? What is the relation of the church to the arts? In Asher's case, the clash is inevitable

3. Lucas McFadden, "Freedom of Expression: The Plight of Wheaton Artists," *The Record*, September 27, 2002, 6–7.

because painting is simply not allowed in Hasidic Judaism. But the problem goes much deeper for most Christians. It has to do with the contours of the art world as we know it today—and here I am referring to the world of "fine art"—as well as how the art world relates (or, for that matter, *doesn't* relate) to the church. As things stand, there is somewhat of an estrangement of the art world from the church. Of course, it wasn't always this way: one has only to think of how much art in Western history has been quite explicitly Christian and even designed to be placed in churches. Yet, despite the common assumption that the way we think about art and the role it plays in society has "always been this way," it actually hasn't. Rather, our ideas about art are only a couple of centuries old, for the most part, even though they have their roots in the Renaissance—which means that, once upon a time, people thought very differently about art.

For the moment, we need to consider the art world as it stands today. And here it is helpful to turn to Michel Foucault's notion of a discourse. While the term "discourse" might sound as if it's about how language is used, Foucault has in mind how any kind of human activity operates—whether it's the world of professional tennis or American politics or the local PTA. Of course, as we noted regarding the term *habitus*, "discourse" can also be replaced with the term "liturgy." For liturgies—just like discourses—establish desired goods, authoritative texts and individuals, and appropriate rituals. A liturgy, in its most basic form, shapes our actions and desires. So, in explicating Foucault's notion of discourse in relation to art, we are really talking about the liturgy of the art world. And that, in turn, will tell us a great deal about liturgy in general.

In his lecture titled "The Order of Discourse," Foucault points out that discourses (and thus liturgies) are ordered by (1) what they exclude or prohibit, (2) how they separate themselves from other discourses, (3) what they take to be their primary texts and what sorts of "commentary" upon them is acceptable, and (4) how everything is guided by ritual and by those who make the decisions as to what can and cannot be said or done.[4] In other words, we all know that there are some things you can or can't do or say, depending on

---

4. This lecture is included as an appendix to Michel Foucault, *The Archaeology of Knowledge*, trans. A. M. Sheridan Smith (New York: Pantheon Books, 1972), 215–37. Strangely, the title of this text in English is "The Discourse on Language."

a given context. We also know that, again depending on the context, there are certain authoritative texts (such as the US Constitution) and persons (such as judges) that state and enforce "the rules." I take Foucault's account to be an excellent description of how discourses actually work. It is *always* the case that discourses have their rules and authorities and rituals.

So how might we apply this to the world of art?

Exclusion and Primary Texts

Let's start with what is excluded or prohibited in the art world. At first glance, it might seem that virtually nothing is prohibited. After all, contemporary artists are known for such outrageous "art" as placing crucifixes in urine (Andres Serrano's *Piss Christ*, 1987) or including elephant dung on a painting (Chris Ofili's *The Holy Virgin Mary*, 1996).[5] Indeed, it would be safe to say that the art world particularly prizes innovation or originality, so much so that artists sometimes turn to extreme tactics to be recognized as truly "innovative." Thus, one thing that is generally excluded or else marginalized in the art world is art that is highly imitative and unoriginal. Such work would either be considered "bad art" or "popular art."

Why is innovation so important? Here it is helpful to turn to the philosopher Immanuel Kant (1724–1804),[6] since he was one of the most influential thinkers in framing the modern paradigm. In fact, most of us don't know how much we've been (usually indirectly) influenced by Kant's thinking about art. A phrase we can use to unpack his account is his claim that "beautiful art is the art of genius."[7] To get to what he means by fine (beautiful) art, let's consider Kant's conception of "genius."

But first, a couple points of comparison on the notion of "genius": In 1746, the French theorist Charles Batteux (1713–80) had argued that art was all about *imitating* nature, and the "genius"

5. The latter piece was the subject of an infamous lawsuit by the then mayor of New York City, Rudi Giuliani, when it was exhibited in 1999 at the Brooklyn Museum of Art.

6. Given that this chapter and the next are concerned with our ways of thinking about art, I include historical dates to give a better idea of when those ideas came about.

7. Immanuel Kant, *Critique of the Power of Judgment*, trans. Paul Guyer and Eric Matthews (Cambridge: Cambridge University Press, 2000), §46.

is the one who is a superb *imitator*.[8] This conception of genius is easy enough to understand, for such a genius is essentially someone who has learned the techniques of a given type of art form and has become a highly developed craftsman. Johann Sebastian Bach (1685–1750) seems to have held such a view, given his comment: "I worked hard. Anyone who works as hard as I did can achieve the same results."[9] Bach is surely overstating the case (in a very modest and humble sort of way), but his viewpoint is clear enough: one becomes an artist by becoming a craftsman. Yet consider how different is the following description of the genius, given by William Duff (1732–1815) in 1770:

> A man of genius is really a kind of different being from the rest of the species. The bent of his disposition, the complexion of his temper, the general turn of his character, his passions and his pursuits are for the most part very dissimilar from those of the bulk of mankind. Hence partly it happens that his manners appear ridiculous to some and disagreeable to others.[10]

Here, in contrast, we have a portrait of the artist as rather different from you and me. The artist is some rather strange person—either "ridiculous" or "disagreeable"—who isn't like "the rest of the species." Someone like Vincent van Gogh comes to mind. Or how about the German artist Joseph Beuys (1921–86)? His performance art includes *How to Explain Pictures to a Dead Hare* (1965), in which his head is covered in gold leaf and honey, one foot covered in felt and the other in iron: for two hours, he walks around an art gallery carrying a dead hare and explains to it the meaning of the art. Another of his performance pieces is titled *I Like America and America Likes Me* (1974, René Block Gallery, New York City), which consists of him spending several days in a gallery with a felt blanket (note: felt is a recurring theme in his art), a flashlight, a live coyote, and copies of the *Wall Street Journal* delivered daily. In the case of Beuys, it's hard *not* to come to the conclusion that he's not quite like the rest of the species.

8. Charles Batteux, *Les beaux arts réduits à un même principe* (Paris: Durand, 1746).
9. This is a quotation widely attributed to Bach.
10. William Duff, *Critical Observations on the Writings of the Most Celebrated Original Geniuses in Poetry* (London: T. Becket and P. A. De Hont, 1770), 339.

As it turns out, Kant gives us a picture of the genius that is a lot closer to Duff's than Batteux's. According to Kant in his *Critique of the Power of Judgment* (1790), "the genius is a favorite of nature, the likes of which one has to regard as only a rare phenomenon."[11] But what *is* genius? Kant tells us that "genius is a *talent* for producing that for which no determinate rule can be given . . . consequently that *originality* must be its primary characteristic."[12] Whereas Batteux had stressed being a good imitator, Kant goes in the radically opposite direction: being as original as possible. You might say that the "rules" don't apply to the genius.[13] As Kant puts it, "everyone agrees that genius is entirely opposed to the *spirit of imitation*."[14] Thus, the genius's artworks become examples for lesser artists (poor saps!) to imitate, while great artists somehow just come up with great ideas. Kant's concept of genius gets even more interesting when he claims that "the author of a product that he owes to his genius does not know himself how the ideas for it come to him."[15] This clearly separates the genius artist from the scientist, at least for Kant. Whereas the genius artist has absolutely no idea of how she came up with her ideas, says Kant, a scientist like Newton can explain each of the steps that led him to his theory. So creating for the genius is a kind of mysterious process that even *she* does not understand, unlike Bach's view in which it can be more or less explained by the techniques of a craftsman who's at the top of his game. To sum up Kant's account, then, (1) true geniuses are original, (2) what they create is exemplary for everyone else, and (3) they are unable to explain how they created their masterpieces. Accordingly, the true primary texts of the art world are those that are original and thus exemplary. They are first and foremost *innovative*. Other works of art—works that are derivative in one sense

11. Kant, *Critique of the Power of Judgment*, §49.

12. Ibid., §46.

13. As the quotation from Kant makes clear, "genius is a *talent*" according to Kant. If we were to pursue this carefully defined conception of genius, then Kant's view might be less problematic. However, elsewhere Kant speaks of the genius not as a talent but as a person ("the product of a genius . . . is an example not for imitation . . . but for emulating by another genius," *Critique of the Power of Judgment*, §49). Moreover, I am less interested in explicating exactly what Kant thought and more on how Kant has normally been interpreted.

14. Ibid., §47. I should point out that Kant often uses phrases like "on this point everyone agrees" precisely when he is putting forth ideas on which everyone does *not* agree.

15. Ibid., §46.

or another—count more like secondary texts or as commentaries on the primary texts.

Think about some of the primary artists of the art world: poets like Homer or T. S. Eliot (1888–1965); playwrights like William Shakespeare (1564–1616) or Samuel Beckett (1906–89); painters like Leonardo da Vinci (1452–1519) or Picasso (1881–1973); composers like Ludwig van Beethoven (1770–1827) or Gioacchino Rossini (1792–1868); sculptors like Michelangelo (1475–1564) or Auguste Rodin (1840–1917); photographers like Edward Weston (1886–1958) or Ansel Adams (1902–84); filmmakers like Alfred Hitchcock (1899–1980) or François Truffaut (1932–84). What are the "primary texts" of the art world? Homer's *Odyssey*, Eliot's *The Waste Land* (1922), Shakespeare's *Hamlet* (1600/1601), Beckett's *Waiting for Godot* (1948–49), da Vinci's *Mona Lisa* (1503–6), Beethoven's *Fifth Symphony* (1804–8), Rossini's *The Barber of Seville* (1816), Michelangelo's *David* (1501–4), Rodin's *The Thinker* (1902), Weston's *Pepper* (1930), Adams's *Clearing Winter Storm* (1935), Hitchcock's *North by Northwest* (1959), and Truffaut's *The 400 Blows* (1959). That is a mere sampling of some of the "great" artists who have become exemplary for others, a list that is hardly inclusive or exhaustive.[16] There are certainly other artists who could be added to this list of primary artists and their "texts." And then we would need to begin the somewhat messy process of deciding who counts as a "primary" artist and who is a mere "secondary" artist. But getting all that exactly right hardly matters here.

Now, there is something *right* about Kant's idea of the genius: one somehow gets ideas, and it is not always clear where those ideas come from. The literature on creativity or innovation (and whether they are one phenomenon or two) is vast and, understandably, contradictory. For creativity is hardly easy to explain: there is something mysterious about it. At least as far back as Plato (428–348 BC), in the dialogue *Ion*, there has been the question of exactly *where* artists (or, in this particular case, poets) get their ideas. Speaking to the poet named Ion, who has just returned from Epidaurus having won first prize for reciting Homer, Socrates suggests that his "skill" really results from his being "out of his mind." Socrates says, "This gift you have of speaking well on Homer is not an art; it is a power

16. Since the "art world" is largely a Western construct, I limit myself here to Western examples.

divine . . . so the lyric poets are not in their senses when they make these lovely lyric poems."[17] Ion is not at all convinced that Socrates is right,[18] but this idea that poets are divinely inspired has been widely held, as has been the notion that somehow artists just get ideas in some sort of magical way. No more influential expression of this idea of creation exists than that from a famous letter attributed to none other than Wolfgang Amadeus Mozart (1756–91).

> Concerning my way of composing . . . I can really say no more on this subject than the following; for I myself know no more about it, and cannot account for it. When I am, as it were, completely myself, entirely alone, and of good cheer—say, travelling in a carriage, or walking after a good meal, or during the night when I cannot sleep; it is on such occasions that my ideas flow best and most abundantly. *Whence* and *how* they come, I know not; nor can I force them. . . . When I proceed to write down my ideas, I take out of the bag of my memory . . . what has previously been collected into it. . . . For this reason the committing to paper is done quickly enough, for everything is, as I said before, already finished; and it rarely differs on paper from what it was in my imagination.[19]

There is something so gloriously "romantic" about this account that it is almost painful to discover that it is a pure fabrication by Friedrich Rochlitz, who was both a fan of Mozart and had been deeply influenced by Kant's notion of the genius. Rochlitz's account of Mozart's composition process is how he *wanted* it to go. It is as if we *want* artists to be capable of something like magical power. The contemporary philosopher Jerrold Levinson goes so far as to say that

> the whole tradition of art assumes art is creative in the strict sense, that it is a godlike activity in which the artist brings into being what did not exist beforehand—much as a demiurge forms a world out of inchoate matter. . . . There is a special aura that envelops composers, as well as other artists, because we think of them as true creators.[20]

17. *Ion* 533d–534a, in Plato, *The Collected Dialogues*, ed. Edith Hamilton and Huntington Cairns (Princeton: Princeton University Press, 1961).

18. *Ion* 536d–e.

19. Quoted in Maynard Solomon, "On Beethoven's Creative Process: A Two-Part Invention," in *Beethoven Essays* (Cambridge, MA: Harvard University Press, 1988), 129.

20. Jerrold Levinson, "What a Musical Work Is," in *Music, Art, & Metaphysics: Essays in Philosophical Aesthetics* (Ithaca, NY: Cornell University Press, 1990), 66–67.

While we have already seen that it is far too much to say that "the *whole* tradition of art" has held this view, it clearly has held sway for more or less the last couple of centuries (that is, during the "modern" or "romantic" period).

The Transformation of the Status of the Artist

Seeing the artist as genius has consequences, and quite problematic ones. First, the genius myth has promoted the idea of the artist as some sort of "lone creator" who neither needs nor wants the influence of or interaction with others—the artist off alone in a garret. Augusto Boal speaks of "the solitary author locked in his study, to whom divine inspiration dictated a finished text."[21] Second, whereas artists had generally been seen as craftsmen (Bach's view of himself was largely the view held throughout Western history), now they became "godlike." For instance, Wilhelm Heinrich Wackenroder (1773–98) and Ludwig Tieck (1773–1853) speak of artists as "a few chosen men whom [God] has anointed as His favorites."[22] Composer George Bizet (1838–75) goes so far as to say that "Beethoven is not a human, he is a god."[23] Composer Carl Maria von Weber demands that the composer become "free as a god."[24] Lest one think that this way of thinking is simply one common to musicians or to the nineteenth century, one need only consider what two more recent artists have said of themselves. When Henri Matisse was working on his famed chapel for Benedictine nuns in Vence (France), one of the nuns asked him for whom he was building such a structure. He replied that he was doing it for God. Later, Matisse said to that same nun: "I am doing it for myself." She responded, "But you told me you were doing it for God." And Matisse answered, "Yes, but I *am* God."[25] Or consider how the playwright and Broadway director

21. Augusto Boal, *Theatre of the Oppressed*, trans. Charles A. and Maria-Odilia Leal McBride (New York: Theatre Communications Group, 1985), 134.

22. Wilhelm Heinrich Wackenroder and Ludwig Tieck, *Outpourings of an Art-Loving Friar*, trans. Edward Mornin (New York: Frederick Ungar, 1975), 59.

23. Walter Salmen, "Social Obligations of the Emancipated Musician in the 19th Century," in *The Social Status of the Professional Musician from the Middle Ages to the 19th Century*, trans. Herbert Kaufman and Barbara Reisner (New York: Pendragon, 1983), 269.

24. Ibid., 270.

25. Janet Hobhouse, *The Bride Stripped Bare: The Artist and the Female Nude in the Twentieth Century* (New York: Weidenfeld & Nicolson, 1988), 102.

Arthur Laurents describes writers: he calls them "the chosen people," a phrase reminiscent of Kant's idea of the genius as nature's favorite.[26] In any case, artists take on an exalted status, becoming something like special agents of God or else simply gods themselves. The contemporary Christian composer Rory Noland puts this as follows:

> Artists were now more than mere mortals. For the first time in history, a successful artist was more likely than a scholar, priest, or scientist to be labeled a genius. The artistic temperament was viewed as a wild-eyed, mysterious, godlike quality bestowed on a chosen few who were then capable of doing superhuman things. Artists were not of this world, people thought, but above and beyond it, which explains why all sorts of eccentric, antisocial, and immoral behavior on their part was not only overlooked, but was actually celebrated.[27]

One could cite Beethoven, Picasso, or a variety of other artists whose behavior—either scandalous or unreasonable—was tolerated by patrons and friends because these artists were considered to be above mere mortals. Of course, it's one thing to say that God is the giver of talents that allow us to make art; it's quite another thing to say that the artist is thereby somehow like or equal to God.

Yet this idea that artists are like God in some way deserves further inspection. What would it *mean* to say that an artist is like God? In effect, Kant's genius is a godlike character, for the genius creates seemingly out of nothing—*creatio ex nihilo*. Where nothing exists, suddenly a masterpiece comes into being. The genius, then, is like the God of Christianity. I will return to the theological aspect of this change more fully in the next chapter. Yet here we need to consider how much this idea alters our conception of the artist.

In effect, the resulting conception is that of a highly exalted figure. This move puts the artist in a difficult situation: suddenly the artist is now greatly above the audience. Given such a lofty perch, artists sometimes do not feel any need to speak to a general audience. Instead, artistic practice becomes something that one does for *oneself*. Of course, the problem was that artists have sometimes wanted it both ways in terms of being understood and appreciated. A lack of understanding or appreciation by the audience has come

26. Robert Berkvist, "Arthur Laurents, Playwright and Director on Broadway, Dies at 93," *New York Times*, May 6, 2011, B10.
27. Rory Noland, *The Heart of the Artist* (Grand Rapids: Zondervan, 1999), 364.

to be interpreted as a sign of greatness: according to the myth that started to take shape in the nineteenth century, innovative artists are those whose genius is not sufficiently appreciated. Thus, art that is immediately and universally enjoyed has come to be seen as somehow aesthetically inferior. Today this "myth of the unappreciated genius" has gained such a hold that we tend to assume that it has always been the norm for great artists not to be sufficiently appreciated by their contemporaries, despite the fact that there is ample evidence to suggest that this is only true in certain cases.[28] We tend to assume that—by definition—a truly great work of art is one that initially meets with great resistance or else is simply ignored. Again, Van Gogh is the poster boy for that idea. In any case, this way of thinking about the artistic genius has proved extremely useful: artists who have not been popular (or at least have felt that they did not receive the attention they deserved) could always take solace in the idea that such is the lot of great geniuses, and that artists who happen to be popular are simply "selling out." Of course, no doubt there *are* artists who "sell out" in some sense or another. We'll consider this phenomenon in chapter 4. Moreover, artists are not always fully appreciated in their time, and those of us who consider ourselves to be "artists" in the more exclusive sense of the term are often bothered by that. Yet, with some notable exceptions, the great artists of the past that we celebrate today were generally celebrated as great artists by their contemporaries.

Artistic Ritual and Authority in the Art World

Yet what about the other half of the phrase "beautiful art is the art of genius?" For Kant, what distinguishes both fine art and *judgments* about fine art is *purity*. Perhaps the most important idea of artistic purity is that both art objects and our judgments about these objects are connected to neither purpose nor rationality. This is not just a minor break with the previous conception of art, but one of cataclysmic importance. According to Kant, when we make aesthetic judgments (like "this object is beautiful"), we must do so in a way that is purely "disinterested." Kant gives us a rather politically

28. See Hans Lenneberg, "The Myth of the Unappreciated (Musical) Genius," *Musical Quarterly* 66 (1980): 219–31.

incorrect example of what he is *not* talking about: in 1666, a group of Iroquois visited Paris, and instead of enjoying the beauty of the grand buildings and artwork on display, they were drawn to the rotisseries full of meat.[29] Or, to give a different example, there's a Dutch still life of a banquet of food in the Art Institute of Chicago that's located in a place I often reach around lunchtime (assuming I arrive when the museum opens). It's called "Still Life" and was painted by Pieter Claesz (1597/98–1660). As long as I admire and appreciate that painting for its *form* (and that alone), I am making a purely aesthetic judgment. However, if the food looks particularly attractive to me, then I've moved away from a purely *aesthetic* judgment to one that is interested in the subject matter—I'm now enjoying it because the food looks tasty. So here we have a very strong prohibition: according to Kant, a true aesthetic judgment can have nothing to do with any practical desires but must remain pure. This means that art can be put to only *one* "use"—the purely aesthetic use of contemplation.[30] My gazing at that painting (no matter how hungry I am) must be "merely *contemplative*" and "*devoid of all interest.*"[31] That purity even extends to *reason*: if we consider an art object to be "good," then we are applying a rational category to it and assuming that it has some kind of end or purpose. Thus, a vase can be "good" if it works well for holding flowers (it fulfills its function). But, if we look at it "aesthetically," our aesthetic judgment regarding the vase can't take its function into account (and one could argue that a vase is inherently compromised as an art object because it can have a practical use). Kant insists that works of art must have no purpose: they are to be created for no other purpose than to be admired *aesthetically*. This is why he says that "flowers, free designs, lines aimlessly intertwined in each other under the name of foliage" are particularly exemplary as works of art, for it is hard to see any "purpose" in a flower, which just *is*.[32] In effect, Kant removes art from the world of wants and desires, the world of ethics, and the world of rationality. An artwork must not be created for any purpose *except* that of being an art object: something to look at and admire. To explain this rarefied sense of

29. Kant, *Critique of the Power of Judgment*, §2.

30. Nicholas Wolterstorff has done a masterful job of critiquing the ideal of aesthetic contemplation in his book *Art in Action* (Grand Rapids: Eerdmans, 1980).

31. Kant, *Critique of the Power of Judgment*, §53.

32. Ibid., §4.

"use," Kant gives us the idea of a *purposiveness* that is "without representation of an end."[33] What he means by this is that artworks should only have the "purpose" of being art and that means being something that is pleasant aesthetically.

Practically, the implications of Kant's move here are highly significant. If art is not connected to rationality, then it literally has nothing "to say." Although it was not Kant who claimed that art was about expressing emotions or even "expressing oneself," it is not hard to see how Kant's insistence that art be detached from rationality could very easily lead to those very typical ideas of the romantic or modern paradigm. The role of the artist is to create, not to make moral judgments. In the famed preface to *The Picture of Dorian Gray*, Oscar Wilde states a number of things that naturally follow from Kant's insistence that art have no ethical "point" to make.

> The artist is the creator of beautiful things. . . . There is no such thing as a moral or an immoral book. Books are well written, or badly written. That is all. . . . No artist desires to prove anything. . . . No artist has ethical sympathies. An ethical sympathy in an artist is an unpardonable mannerism of style. . . . All art is quite useless.[34]

Although not all artists would go as far as Wilde does, the freedom that Kant's view brought has been generally welcomed. Of course, a particularly problematic historical aspect of Kant's view is that art, having been entirely severed from reason, could no longer say anything that could be called "true." Unlike philosophy or science, then, art could no longer be taken seriously as *rational*.

But this also meant that there was now a tension between the art world and the church. Almost from its beginning, the church has employed the arts. True, the arts have been appreciated by the church for being *beautiful*, but those stained-glass windows of Chartres were designed to tell the Christian story. The church has a long history of using art for very practical purposes. Later, we will consider the extent to which this is acceptable, for there is

---

33. Ibid., §17.

34. Oscar Wilde, *The Picture of Dorian Gray: An Annotated, Uncensored Edition* (Cambridge, MA: Belknap, 2011), 273. This controversial preface first appeared in the 1891 edition of the novel, and it was written to address Wilde's critics. Today, the preface is seen as a *locus classicus* for the idea of "art for art's sake."

an opposite worry: does the church tend to view art from a purely utilitarian perspective? In any case, the purity of art and its disconnection from both the good (ethics) and the true puts the art world and the church at odds, and complicates things for any artist who is a Christian.

There is a further aspect in which aesthetic judgments are to be pure, and it is one that is, at least at first, a little hard to grasp. Kant insists that anything that is truly beautiful not only *must* be liked (aesthetically) but *will* be liked by *everyone*. Says Kant: "the judgment of taste ascribes assent to everyone."[35] This is almost the equivalent (said, of course, with a pseudo-German accent) of, "You vill look at zee painting, and you vill like it!" Kant's insistence here is odd in more than one respect. According to him, the reason we judge something to be beautiful has nothing to do with the object and everything to do with us. In other words, we pronounce something beautiful on the basis of what happens in *us*, not on the basis of the object itself. So our pronouncement is purely *subjective*. Yet, since Kant thinks that all human beings have similar rational powers, we should likewise all agree regarding the beauty of any given piece of art. Thus, Kant's view is that our judgments about art are *subjective* but are still *universal* and *necessary*. That is, we fully expect others to agree with us. On Kant's view, if I think a particular painting is beautiful, you should agree with me (assuming, of course, that our sensory systems are operating correctly).

It's not hard to see that there is a problem with Kant's idea of what it means for an object to be beautiful. On the one hand, Kant's theory makes beauty purely subjective rather than objective: the beauty of an object doesn't depend on the object itself but only on the person perceiving it. C. S. Lewis (1898–1963) makes reference to a school textbook that, out of charity to the authors, he simply refers to as *The Green Book*. The authors of the text tell the familiar story of Samuel Taylor Coleridge (1772–1834), who hears two tourists describing a waterfall. One describes it as "sublime," the other as "pretty." Although Coleridge agrees with the one who calls it "sublime," the authors of *The Green Book* make the point that both statements simply reflect the feelings of the persons, not the waterfall itself. Such is Kant's view. Even the authors of *The Green*

---

35. Kant, *Critique of the Power of Judgment*, §19.

Book realize that this view in effect trivializes aesthetic judgments. As they put it: "We appear to be saying something very important about something: and actually we are only saying something about our own feelings."[36] This is a view that is deeply at odds with the entire history of theologians who have thought and written about beauty, not to mention what most people have traditionally meant in saying, "This painting is beautiful."

On the other hand, aesthetic judgments are quite unlike typical judgments. Whereas we generally make judgments about things on the basis of their *purpose*, Kant explicitly says that purpose has nothing to do with art. As long as one is committed to the idea that human experience of aesthetic objects is universally the same, it is possible to hold that aesthetic judgments are universal and necessary. But, in our time, such an assumption seems very hard to hold. It might be easier to hold if we were to say that there is something about the *object* that makes it beautiful, but placing everything upon the subject very quickly leads to a kind of aesthetic relativism that can either be somewhat limited or full blown.[37] Although aesthetic relativism is quite common in our era, it is profoundly at odds both with what the Bible itself says and with the Christian tradition. We may not always agree on the beauty of any particular object (a subject to which we will return), but it seems strange to say that the beauty (or value) of art is purely relative to whoever happens to behold it.

Art "Experts" and the Highbrow/Lowbrow Distinction

Consider what all this means *practically* in the art world. Given the problem of aesthetic judgments being subjective, it is not hard to see why the art world relies on "experts" to "declare" the value of art. That world of experts is a relatively small one, composed largely of art critics, museum curators, gallery owners, art teachers, and the artists themselves. Tom Wolfe (1931–) calls such experts "culturati" and says:

36. C. S. Lewis, *The Abolition of Man* (New York: Macmillan, 1947), 1–2. *The Green Book* is actually Alec King and Martin Ketley, *The Control of Language: A Critical Approach to Reading and Writing* (London: Longmans, Green, 1939).

37. I find it interesting that my students, who normally are strongly against ethical relativism, are often aesthetic relativists to some degree or another.

If it were possible to make such a diagram of the art world, we would see that it is made up of (in addition to the artists) about 750 culturati in Rome, 500 in Milan, 1,750 in Paris, 1,250 in London, 2,000 in Berlin, Munich, and Düsseldorf, 3,000 in New York, and perhaps 1,000 scattered about the rest of the known world. That is the art world, approximately 10,000 souls—a mere hamlet!—restricted to *les beaux mondes* of eight cities.[38]

One might find this a crass oversimplification of the art world and exactly who belongs to it. One might quibble with the numbers or the exact set of cities. Yet it's rather hard to argue with the overall point, that there are a relatively small number of "experts" in the art world who decide who's in and who's out. I'm very sorry to say this, but *you*—gentle reader—are probably not (and how can one say this nicely enough in our politically correct age?) in the in-group. Of course, I know I'm definitely not in there either, so we're in the same boat (it's a very big boat, with ample room for all the "non-culturati"). So there are those who are "in," those who are "out," and those "on the fringe." What camp a given artist is in can be defined by where her artworks are exhibited. Do they make it to one of the major art galleries (in New York City, they're mainly in Chelsea)? Do they make it to one of the major museums in the world? Are they played by major orchestras or noted ensembles or at important music festivals? Are they screened at important film festivals (like Cannes or Sundance)?

That last question, the one about films, leads us to a further difficulty, since most films don't, by this definition, fall into the category of fine art. Note that the art world is composed of "fine art" rather than "popular art." One could just as well use the distinction of "highbrow" and "lowbrow" art. But both of these distinctions are more problematic than they might seem. Consider Lawrence W. Levine's conversation with a scholar who had just seen and come to admire some films by Buster Keaton (1895–1966). When Levine exclaims that "Keaton was a great artist," the scholar immediately corrects him by saying, "A great *popular* artist."[39] As a kind of test case, Levine shows how William Shakespeare had—as recently as the nineteenth century—been part of everyday, working-class

---

38. Tom Wolfe, *The Painted Word* (New York: Bantam, 1976), 26.

39. Lawrence W. Levine, *Highbrow/Lowbrow: The Emergence of Cultural Hierarchy in America* (Cambridge, MA: Harvard University Press, 1988), 1.

American culture. Particularly telling is the illustration of Huck and Jim's decision in Mark Twain's *Huckleberry Finn* to make some money by performing parts of Shakespeare's *Romeo and Juliet* and *Richard III*. As Levine puts it: "That the presentation of Shakespeare in small Mississippi River towns could be conceived of as potentially lucrative tells us much about the position of Shakespeare in the nineteenth century."[40] In other words, Shakespeare would have needed to be seen as "popular" literature—and well known to everyday folk—to make performing him even remotely financially successful. Moreover, Shakespeare was performed at that time in all sorts of bowdlerized versions with names like *Julius Sneezer*, *Hamlet and Egglet*, and *Ye Comedie of Errours, a Glorious, Uproarous [sic] Burlesque, Not Indecorous nor Censorous, with Many a Chorus, Warranted Not to Bore Us, Now for the First Time Set before Us*. And I'd be willing to wager that it *didn't* bore the audience. Think of Shakespeare's place today. The various Shakespeare theaters may do a thriving business, but it's not because they are appealing to the masses. While many high school students are introduced to Shakespeare, their normal response is not that this is exciting reading material but that it is simply something they must learn to pass a test. By the twentieth century, Shakespeare had become a rarefied author who had gone from lowbrow to highbrow. But this change was *not* accidental: it was largely engineered. For there were those in high society that thought Shakespeare should be kept from both the lower-class audiences and the actors who would dare take liberties with his texts like the ones mentioned above. As A. A. Lipscomb noted in 1882, Shakespeare "is destined to become the Shakespeare of the college and university, and even more the Shakespeare of private and select culture."[41] Such was the deliberate takeover of Shakespeare from being the property of the masses to that of the elite. And one can only conclude that this move—certainly a "hostile" takeover—was eminently successful.

While the Shakespeare example is rather telling, there are others. It's common knowledge that opera began as a popular and even "vulgar" art form, though it's about as far away from that today as could be imagined. One reason for both Shakespeare and opera

40. Ibid., 13.
41. Ibid., 73.

becoming high art is simply the fact that they are so removed from their time that it takes a certain knowledge and sophistication to appreciate them. In other words, they simply *can't* occupy a space in popular art because so few people can easily "get" them (either in terms of understanding or, especially with opera, in terms of affording them).[42] What about the Beatles? They are clearly popular art, but many people with high artistic sensibilities would see many of their songs as great art. Bob Dylan is even more problematic, since his song "Desolation Row" is included in *The Oxford Book of American Poetry*. Just to clarify things, most "popular" singers are *not* included in such an elite text. That the editors chose to include Dylan's work in a "highbrow" sort of collection is remarkable, but even more remarkable is what they say about him: "The lyrics in three of his record albums from the mid-1960s—*Bringing It All Back Home, Highway 61 Revisited*, and *Blonde on Blonde*—particularly reward close analysis of the sort given to demanding examples of modern poetry."[43] High praise indeed for what is normally classified as "folk music." But this only serves to show that our distinction between highbrow and lowbrow is somewhat artificial and, I would contend, largely created because of snobbery. It serves those who consider themselves and their art to be "highbrow," for it gives them license to dismiss certain kinds of art as "beneath them." I would very much like to say that there is a much less sinister motive at work in making such a distinction, but I simply don't see any such "neutral" motive.[44] We may need something like the highbrow/lowbrow distinction, if only to designate art that has limited appeal from that which has much broader appeal. But we need to realize the implications of this distinction.

42. Of course, if you think about it, it's not too hard to see that current pop culture (whether music or television programs) would likely be just as inaccessible to an audience living three hundred years from now: they wouldn't understand the slang, wouldn't get cultural references, and would find it hard to relate to the kinds of lives being portrayed.

43. David Lehman and John Brehm, eds., *The Oxford Book of American Poetry* (Oxford: Oxford University Press, 2006), 962.

44. Levine reminds us of the rather unsavory origin of the highbrow/lowbrow distinction. Whereas such "aesthetically refined" artists as Shakespeare and Milton literally had high brows, the brows of "inferior races" (one such example being a cannibal from New Zealand) were noticeably short or nonexistent. The distinction was made between the "Civilized" and "Caucasian" as opposed to the "Human Idiot" and the "Bushman." See *Highbrow/Lowbrow*, 222.

Art as Religion and Ritualistic Behavior

Another important—though complicated—aspect is fine art's relation to religion (and thus to the church). If we go back to when the
romantic or modern conception of art was forming—around the
end of the eighteenth and beginning of the nineteenth centuries—we
find that theorists are beginning to see them as connected. Consider
what the composer and writer E. T. A. Hoffmann (1776–1822) says
about instrumental music:

> No art arises so directly from man's spiritual nature, and no art
> calls for such primary, ethereal resources, as music. Sound audibly
> expresses an awareness of the highest and holiest. . . . By virtue of
> its essential character, therefore, music is a form of religious wor-
> ship . . . and its origin is to be sought and found only in religion.[45]

Now, music may well be "a form of religious worship," but Hoffmann is hardly speaking of religion in any traditional sense. What
replaces ancient church music for Hoffmann is the instrumental
music of Joseph Haydn (1732–1809), Wolfgang Amadeus Mozart
(1756–91), and Ludwig van Beethoven (1770–1827), composers
who are not less religious but instead evidence the religiosity of a
"modern age striving for inner spirituality." In other words, their
music (at least according to Hoffmann) was not "religious" (in
the sense of being dedicated to Christianity or any specific sort of
religion) but was somehow connected to "spirituality." Friedrich
Schleiermacher (1768–1834) speaks of the kinship of art and religion, which he claims "stand beside one another like two friendly
souls whose inner affinity, whether or not they equally surmise it,
is nevertheless still unknown to them."[46] Though he never quite
explains exactly how, Schleiermacher believes that art leads us (or
at least has the capacity to lead us) to the religious.

For many, however, art was not seen as an aid to religion but as a
replacement for religion. In his *Kalligone* (1800), Johann Gottfried
Herder (1744–1803) claimed that music was set free when it was

45. E. T. A. Hoffmann, *E. T. A. Hoffmann's Musical Writings*, trans. Martyn Clarke,
ed. David Charlton (Cambridge: Cambridge University Press, 1989), 355.
46. Friedrich Schleiermacher, *On Religion*, trans. Richard Crouter (Cambridge:
Cambridge University Press, 1988), 69.

shown "*religious awe* [*Andacht*]."[47] *Andacht* suggests the kind of religious reverence and veneration one might show a holy object. By suggesting that music should be accorded the same sort of *Andacht* that would previously have been reserved for holy texts or relics of a revered saint, Herder in effect transfers religious expectations onto aesthetic objects. While talking about music in this reverential way would have been considered highly unusual by most of Herder's contemporaries, it is interesting that only two years after the appearance of *Kalligone*, Johann Nikolaus Forkel, in his biography of Bach, suggests that some of Bach's works could be mentioned "only with a kind of holy worship" (a claim that Bach—who wrote the initials S. D. G., standing for *Soli Deo Gloria* [For God's glory alone], on his scores—could never have imagined making).[48] Wackenroder ultimately goes so far as to claim that "music is certainly the ultimate mystery of faith, the mystique, the fully revealed religion."[49] These were not merely theoretical claims; instead, they began to affect artistic practice. Put bluntly, art took over, almost wholly intact, many of the behavioral expectations of religious experience and worship. Consider both the design of concert halls and museums and the behavioral expectations (ritual) that accompany them. Both are places that are dedicated to the religion of art or culture and are designed to create the appropriate sentiment in the visitor—something not so far from pious devotion. It was completely intentional that many art museums and concert halls were given facades vaguely or explicitly reminiscent of Greek temples, for their function is clearly that of a shrine. It was also no accident that concert halls tended to be decorated with the busts or at least the names of the demigods of classical music, giving them the feel of a musical pantheon. What a concert hall provides is a kind of hallowed space that calls for silence. Of course, the *sort* of silence expected is also important. Wackenroder (along with his friend Ludwig Tieck) tells us that "the appreciation of sublime artworks is akin to prayer."[50] Thus, when the character Joseph Berglinger

47. Peter le Hurray and James Day, *Music and Aesthetics in the Eighteenth and Early-Nineteenth Centuries* (Cambridge: Cambridge University Press, 1981), 257.

48. Johann Nikolaus Forkel, *Über Johann Sebastian Bachs Leben, Kunst und Kunstwerke*, ed. Walther Vetter (Kassel: Bärenreiter, 1970), 12.

49. Wilhelm Heinrich Wackenroder, *Werke und Briefe* (Heidelberg: Lambert Schneider, 1967), 251.

50. Wackenroder and Tieck, *Outpourings of an Art-Loving Friar*, 70.

(the art-loving friar) would attend a concert, "he would sit down in a corner . . . and would listen with the same reverence as he did in church—just as silent and motionless."[51] Thus the kind of behavior expected of the concertgoer became that of the devout at mass. And the same could be said of behavior in art museums: even today, one can often almost *feel* a kind of devout reverence when one visits them.

Conclusion

While there are more features to our current liturgical practice of the art world, these are the most important ones. Having both considered and, in many cases, deconstructed many aspects of that liturgy, it's time for *reconstruction*. How should we think of the status of art and artists? What does it mean to make art? What we need is a paradigm for the arts that better reflects art's true nature and how it can be—indeed, *should be*—central to the church. I do not believe that art is some kind of "add-on" that we "indulge" when we happen to have the time and money. Instead, I think art is central to who we are as human beings. God intends us to be artists. Art is part of our being—and should be part of both our individual lives and the very life of the church. Reconstructing an appropriate paradigm for that centrality is what we turn to in chapter 3.

51. Ibid., 107.

3

Improvising like Jazz

It was at a baseball game, when someone handed him a pair of binoculars, that Andrew Stanton suddenly got the idea for what the character WALL-E should look like. He spent the entire next inning looking at the binoculars backwards, twisting them this way and that to simulate various expressions of sadness and joy. Stanton, the director of the film *WALL-E*, had been thinking for years about the idea of a lone robot left to clean up an uninhabitable earth, but it was only in that moment that he figured out how the animated robot should look. That idea came in an instant, but it took quite some time to realize that watching the songs "Put on Your Sunday Clothes" and "It Only Takes a Moment" from the movie version of *Hello, Dolly!* would be just the right songs to teach WALL-E emotion. Figuring out the "voices" of the robot characters took even longer, and it basically required working with Ben Burtt for a year, during which they kept trying out different sounds until they found the ones that worked. Stanton compares the process to trying out paint swatches on the wall. And these were only some of the myriad details that had to be put in place to make the film a reality.[1]

Many artists will instinctively resonate with the process that Stanton went through. Some ideas come in a moment, but many

1. Most of this information comes from a fascinating interview between Stanton and Terry Gross titled "Animations from Life" on the program *Fresh Air* (July 10, 2008).

aspects have to be worked out over days, weeks, months—even years. And those ideas don't usually come by being isolated but by being connected: with other artists, the history of art, friends who inspire you, and the world of everyday life. Often what happens is that you see something—perhaps as mundane as a pair of binoculars—and you suddenly realize how it could be painted or reworked into something that's both similar and different. Or perhaps you hear something—the chirp of a bird, a musical chord, a mechanical device that has a certain rhythm—and you imagine the beginning of a piece of music. That last example was the inspiration for Dr. Seuss to write his first book *And to Think That I Saw It on Mulberry Street!*[2] Those are just two examples of the multifarious ways of improvisation.

An improvising artist is one who does not create *ex nihilo* but very much *from something*. Here it is helpful to turn to the creation account as depicted in Gen. 1.

Consider the following passage:

> In the beginning when God created the heavens and the earth, the earth was a formless void and darkness covered the face of the deep, while a wind from God swept over the face of the waters. Then God said, "Let there be light"; and there was light. And God saw that the light was good; and God separated the light from the darkness. God called the light Day, and the darkness he called Night. And there was evening and there was morning, the first day. (Gen. 1:1–5)

What exactly is God doing here? Further, what is this "beginning" (*re'sit*) and where does it begin? One can say this is a basic question regarding any kind of genesis: at what point can we say that something *begins*? It is significant that the *Oxford English Dictionary* defines "genesis" as "the action of building up from simple or basic elements to more complex ones."[3] For something like that seems to be described here. The earth is described as "a formless void" and "darkness covered the face of the deep" (*tohu vabohu*,

---

2. Theodore Geisel (aka Dr. Seuss) was aboard a ship sailing from France to the States and became entranced by the thrum of the boat engine. The anapestic tetrameter rhythm (two unstressed syllables followed by a stressed syllable) of the motor became the rhythm of the book. My thanks to Daniel Leonard for this example.

3. *The Oxford English Dictionary*, 2nd ed., s.v. "genesis."

or "the depth in the dark"). And then God creates (*bara*). On this account, things are already *in medias res*—into the middle of affairs. That is, there is already something going on, and then God enters the picture.

Yet, even though Ian Barbour claims that "*creation 'out of nothing' is not a biblical concept*," there exists significant evidence to the contrary.[4] In 2 Macc. 7:28, a mother implores her son to "recognize that God did not make them out of things that existed" (as the NRSV has it), or we could translate this phrase simply as "realize that God made them [the world] out of nothing." Gerhard von Rad claims quite simply that "the conceptional formulation *creatio ex nihilo* is first found" in this passage.[5] But one can also point to Ps. 148:5, in which the psalmist writes, "Let them praise the name of the LORD, for he commanded and they were created." Augustine wrestles with the opening verses of Genesis, but then concludes (speaking of God), "You cannot have gone to work like a human craftsman, who forms a material object from some material in accordance with his imaginative decision. . . . Is there anything that exists at all, if not because of you? Clearly, then, you spoke and things were made. By your word you made them."[6]

While all of this raises some distinctly *theological* questions, my concern here is not with theology but with the artistic ramifications of the notion of *creatio ex nihilo* (creation out of nothing). Gerhard May is certainly right when he states, "Church theology wants through the proposition *creatio ex nihilo* to express and safeguard the omnipotence and freedom of God acting in history."[7] At issue, then, are *power* and *freedom*. The God who can create *ex nihilo* is simply more powerful and free than the God who merely creates from that which already exists. How we interpret the first few verses of the book of Genesis depends very much upon what kind of God we think is being depicted here. A truly powerful God has no need of existent matter. Likewise, a truly powerful artist is

4. Ian Barbour, *Issues in Science and Religion* (Englewood Cliffs, NJ: Prentice-Hall, 1966), 384.

5. Gerhard von Rad, *Old Testament Theology*, vol. 1, trans. D. M. G. Stalker (New York: Harper & Row, 1962), 142.

6. Augustine, *Confessions*, trans. Maria Boulding (Hyde Park, NY: New City, 1997), 11.5.7.

7. Gerhard May, *Creatio Ex Nihilo: The Doctrine of "Creation out of Nothing" in Early Christian Thought*, trans. A. S. Worrall (Edinburgh: T&T Clark, 1994), 180.

one that has no need of tradition and interaction with predecessors. Just as pseudo-Mozart wrote of getting ideas from nowhere, so the romantic artist creates seemingly out of nothing.

As it turns out, most ancient accounts of creation assume *ex nihilo nihil fit*—from nothing comes nothing. Thus, the creation accounts found in various ancient Mesopotamian texts are about creation from *something*. Similarly, early Christian theologians such as Justin Martyr generally were in favor of the "from something" account. That is likewise the view of the pre-Socratic philosopher Parmenides, who believes nothingness or nonbeing makes no sense and so one cannot even say, "It is or it is not." On his account, one can only say, "It is or . . . ," since "nothing" makes no sense. It *is* not. It is *no thing*. Indeed, even that great songwriting team Rogers and Hammerstein point out that "nothing comes from nothing, nothing ever could."

Regarding the account of creation as found in the Old Testament, Catherine Keller speaks of the "mystery of the missing chaos."[8] How, she asks, have theologians simply forgotten about that chaos? The goal of her book *Face of the Deep: A Theology of Becoming* is to deconstruct *ex nihilo* theology and return to that forgotten chaos. Writing as a feminist theologian, she claims that the *ex nihilo* account is a highly *masculine* one. As we have seen, it belongs to a discourse of power. In its place, Keller suggests a theology of *becoming* in which we rethink the very notion of *beginning*. In this respect, she is indebted to Edward Said, who distinguishes between "beginning" and "origin." Whereas beginnings are "secular, humanly produced and ceaselessly re-examined," origins are "divine, mythical and privileged."[9] There is something special about an origin. Keller's problem with *ex nihilo* is that it erases the deep and the past. It speaks only of a moment. And it passes over the chaos out of which creation takes place. To quote Keller, "What if we begin instead to read the Word from the vantage point of its own fecund multiplicity, its flux into flesh, its overflow?"[10]

Keller claims that we begin amid the chaos and the flux. In this respect, the verb means something other than at least one definition

8. Catherine Keller, *Face of the Deep: A Theology of Becoming* (London: Routledge, 2003), chapter 1.

9. Edward Said, *Beginnings: Intention and Method* (New York: Columbia University Press, 1985), xii–xiii.

10. Keller, *Face of the Deep*, 19.

that the *Oxford English Dictionary* provides for "begin"—"take the first step." One never truly *begins*, then, for there is always a step that has already been made. Keller wants to make this point not merely for human beings but also for God. She quotes theologian William P. Brown approvingly: "By and large God does not work *de novo* or *ex nihilo*, but *ex voce* and *per collaborationi* [by collaboration]."[11] To understand what Brown means by this statement, we must return to the Genesis account and note that God works with the earth and the waters in a collaborative way so as to produce animals and sea monsters. God says, "Be fruitful and multiply and fill the waters in the seas" and "Let the earth bring forth living creatures of every kind" (Gen. 1:22, 24).

Justin Martyr writes that "in the beginning [God] of His goodness, for people's sakes, formed all things out of unformed matter."[12] By this account, God orders that which already exists. And that is precisely the problem for the third-century church father Athanasius:

> If this be so, God will be on their theory a Mechanic only, and not a Creator out of nothing; if, that is, He works at existing material, but is not Himself the cause of the material. For He could not in any sense be called Creator unless He is Creator of the material of which the things created have in their turn been made.[13]

But does Athanasius give us a false dilemma? While working on this book, I discovered that a colleague of mine—an Old Testament scholar named John Walton—happens to have a very helpful interpretation of what is being described in Genesis. He insists that we must consider this question: What is the text asserting that God did in this context? As he puts it, the account found in Genesis is not about "the material shape of the cosmos, but rather its functions."[14] In other words, the text isn't about "where does the cosmos come from?" (a question about material) but "why does the cosmos have

11. William P. Brown, *The Ethos of the Cosmos: The Genesis of Moral Imagination in the Bible* (Grand Rapids: Eerdmans, 1999), 41.

12. Justin Martyr, *First Apology* 10 in *St. Justin Martyr: The First and Second Apologies*, trans. Leslie William Barnard (Mahwah, NJ: Paulist Press, 1997), 28.

13. Athanasius, *On the Incarnation* 2.3.4 in *Nicene and Post-Nicene Fathers*, series 1, vol. 4, ed. Philip Schaff and Henry Wace (Buffalo, NY: Christian Literature, 1892), 2.4.

14. John H. Walton, *The Lost World of Genesis One: Ancient Cosmology and the Origins Debate* (Downers Grove, IL: IVP Academic, 2009), 62; *Genesis*, NIV Application Commentary (Grand Rapids: Zondervan, 2001), 71.

the order and structure that it has?" (a question about function). Of course, this also gives us a different idea of creation—by this account, even God works with material that is already there. And Walton argues that this is exactly what is meant by the Hebrew word (*bara*) that we translate as "create." So the issue is not "existence vs. nonexistence" but *order*.[15]

Again, though, my concern here is not theological in nature. I am not trying to make a statement regarding the orthodox version of creation. I leave that to the theologians. Instead, I am asking a question: What does each account tell us about artistic creation? As I see it, *on either view*, God is an improviser. For creation—however we define it—is precisely God setting in motion a reality of "ceaseless alterations" (as Milbank puts it).[16] Thus, the very being of life is improvisatory—by which I mean that it is a mixture of both structure and contingency, of regularity and unpredictability, of constraint and possibility. Further, if God is indeed still at work in the world, then God is likewise part of that improvisatory movement. Living in such a reality means that we take part in that improvisatory movement in all that we do. Since we are creatures embedded in multiple and ever-changing historical and cultural milieus, our identities and very being arise from our relation to others and to the world we inhabit.

So how would this view of God translate into an account of artistic creation? In my view, we end up with what I call *creatio ex improvisatio* (*improvisatio* is a Latin term that only rarely occurs and only after the fifteenth century). Artistic genesis, then, always begins *somewhere*. And that idea is very much exemplified by Baroque music rather than romantic music.

The Play of Improvisation

Romantic music celebrates the original innovative artist. Baroque music does virtually the opposite. Baroque music was much more of a community affair, something one does not alone but with others.

15. Yet we could also say that even though the first chapter of Genesis is only about God bringing order out of chaos, ultimately anything that has come into being must have come into being by way of God.

16. John Milbank, "'Postmodern Critical Augustinianism': A Short *Summa* in Forty-Two Responses to Unasked Questions," in *Modern Theology* 7 (1991): 227.

This was true of how both composers and performers worked, in true improvisatory fashion. David Fuller describes the situation as follows: "A large part of the music of the whole era was sketched rather than fully realized, and the performer had something of the responsibility of a child with a colouring book, to turn these sketches into rounded art-works." Fuller compares the "scores" of Baroque music to the "charts" or "fake books" one finds in jazz.[17] The composer provided some idea of how the piece was to go, but a substantial portion of the shape of the musical piece was up to the performer.

Yet it was not merely the performer who was improvising; it was likewise the composer. Here it is helpful to juxtapose the notion of creation with that of improvisation. By using the term "improvisation" instead of "creation," I mean to stress that artists "fabricate out of what is conveniently on hand" rather than create in the sense of "to produce where nothing was before."[18] In making art, we always *start with something*. The extreme side of such "borrowing" would today come under the rubric of "plagiarism." It may come as rather a surprise that Bach was in the habit of starting with a melody appropriated from either himself or someone else. A well-known example of his creative borrowing is how the popular song "Innsbruch, ich muß dich lassen" ("Innsbruch, I must leave you") morphed into "O Welt, ich muß dich lassen" ("O World, I must leave you") that became part of his *St. Matthew Passion*. Of course, this was standard practice at the time—a time when the idea of ownership of intellectual property didn't exist. George Frederic Handel was also prolific in his "recycling" of his and others' work.[19] This raises questions about the notion of ownership and copyright, to which we will later return.

Such a conception of artistic creation is strikingly at odds with that of the modern/romantic paradigm. Now, I admit that many modern artists both have been and are currently committed to

17. David Fuller, "The Performer as Composer," in *Performance Practice*, vol. 2, ed. Howard Mayer Brown and Stanley Sadie (Houndmills, UK: Macmillan, 1989), 117–18. A "fake book" provides the performer with chord symbols and the melody, with the expectation that the performer "fake" the rest.

18. See *Merriam-Webster's Collegiate Dictionary*, 11th ed., s.v. "improvise," and *The Oxford English Dictionary*, 2nd ed., s.v. "create."

19. For more on Handel's composing, see John T. Winemiller, "Recontextualizing Handel's Borrowing," *Journal of Musicology* 15 (1997): 444–70.

"pushing the envelope." What I'm questioning is just how "original" even the most supposed "original" pieces of art actually are. I fully admit that, say, Pablo Picasso's painting *Les Desmoiselles d'Avignon* (1907) and the Beatles album *Sgt. Pepper* (1967) are landmark—even in ways *original*—artistic contributions. Yet it strikes me that these examples are nothing like a "complete departure" from their respective genres but are instead a *significant advance* within them. That is to say, they are still *part* of a recognizable genre and not something entirely new—which indicates that they all represent semi-new ways of reworking what already existed. Thus, I am contending that the old wisdom of Ecclesiastes still holds: "there is nothing new under the sun" (Eccles. 1:9). Without a doubt, there is reworking, revision, rethinking, and renewal—but there is no true *revolution*. Here I side with Gadamer, who writes, "Even where life changes violently, as in ages of revolution, far more of the old is preserved in the supposed transformation of everything than anyone knows, and it combines with the new to create a new value."[20] Rock 'n' roll may be a new genre, but it could *never* have come into existence without heavy borrowing from the blues.

Gadamer's concept of "play" (*Spiel*) also goes a good ways toward helping us think about how artistic improvisation takes place. Play might seem to be merely something we do as recreation, but Gadamer suggests that play gives us a clue to human activity in general. Note that the German term *Spiel* can be translated into English as either "play" or "game." If we take the latter meaning, we can say that to play is to take part in an activity that exists apart from the single player. Gadamer thinks of the making of art as beginning in the to-and-fro of play but ending in what he calls "*transformation into structure*."[21] At some point, what was the play of experimentation starts to become more "stable" as a structure. The beginning of a musical phrase turns into a full melody. Some lines hastily drawn on a canvas get more and more definition as other lines are drawn. A piece of stone moves from being a square block to an increasingly defined shape. But how does all of this happen? Here there can be no simple answer, for pieces of art come

20. Hans-Georg Gadamer, *Truth and Method*, trans. Joel Weinsheimer and Donald G. Marshall, 2nd rev. ed. (New York: Continuum, 1989), 281.
21. Ibid., 110.

into existence in different ways over varying lengths of time. Gustav Mahler's (1860–1911) first symphony is interesting in this respect. While Mahler wrote the bulk of it in 1888, parts of it come from material dating back to the 1870s, and he revised it more than once. The final version dates to 1906.

While it is difficult to present anything like "the" model for artistic improvisation, consider the following story. Malcolm Cowley gives us what are in effect two descriptions of the process of how Hart Crane (1899–1932) wrote his poetry. According to the first description, a Sunday afternoon party at which everyone was laughing, playing croquet, and having a good time was often the backdrop for his writing. Crane would be among those laughing—and drinking—the most until he would disappear into the next room. With a Cuban rumba or torch song or Ravel's *Bolero* in the background, the partygoers would hear the keys of a typewriter busily banging away. Then, about an hour later, Crane would appear with a poem and have the partygoers read it. At least, that is the way in which Cowley originally told the story. It certainly is intriguing and fits rather well with the artistic genius idea we noted in chapter 2. Yet Cowley later realized that this was really only part of the story. Usually Crane had been thinking about that poem—seemingly produced in an hour—for months or years and writing bits and pieces along the way. Then he would use the occasion of the party to try to "get inspired." But the process of writing the poem wouldn't end there:

> As for the end of the story, it might be delayed for a week or a month. Painfully, persistently—and dead sober—Hart would revise his new poem, clarifying the images, correcting the meter and searching for the right word hour after hour. "The seal's wide spindrift gaze toward paradise," in the second of his "Voyages," was the result of a search that lasted for several days. At first he had written, "The seal's *findrinny* gaze toward paradise," but someone had objected that he was using a non-existent word. Hart and I worked in the same office that year, and I remember his frantic searches through *Webster's Unabridged* and the big *Standard*, his trips to the library— on office time—and his reports of consultations with old sailors in South Street speakeasies. "Findrinny" he could never find, but after paging through the dictionary again he decided that "spindrift" was almost as good and he declaimed the new line exultantly. Even

after one of his manuscripts had been sent to *Poetry* or the *Dial* and perhaps had been accepted, he would still have changes to make.[22]

It strikes me that Crane's experience in writing poetry is probably rather similar to that of the process of how many or even most artistic pieces come into existence. One gets perhaps an inchoate idea, then begins to see it take shape (by either writing some preliminary lines or putting together chords and melodic motifs or taking some pictures or trying out some dance steps). Slowly, not infrequently with painstaking decision making and trial and error, something is transformed into a kind of structure—something that starts to have its own identity.

That is not to say that some pieces of art don't ever come about in a flash of inspiration. Yet even these sorts of stories often turn out to be untrue, or not quite as dramatic as they first seem. Coleridge's poem "Kubla Khan" would seem to be an example to balance that of Crane. After all, here is what he tells us in the preface to the poem:

> On awaking he [Coleridge] appeared to himself to have a distinct recollection of the whole, and taking his pen, ink, and paper, instantly and eagerly wrote down the lines that are here preserved. At this moment he was unfortunately called out by a person on business from Porlock, and detained by him above an hour, and on his return to his room, found, to his no small surprise and mortification, that though he still retained some vague and dim recollection of the general purport of the vision, yet, with the exception of some eight or ten scattered lines and images, all the rest had passed away.[23]

As appealing as this story is, it unravels rather quickly. We know that Coleridge had been reading Samuel Purchas's *Purchas His Pilgrimage* (1617), and it turns out that the first two lines of "Kubla Khan" come, with only a little alteration, directly from a sentence in Purchas.[24] So the poem doesn't come out of "a dream." Indeed,

22. Malcolm Cowley, *Exile's Return: A Literary Odyssey of the 1920s* (New York: Viking, 1951), 229–30.

23. Samuel Taylor Coleridge, "Kubla Khan" in *The Collected Works of Samuel Taylor Coleridge, Poetical Works I*, ed. J. C. C. Mays (Princeton: Princeton University Press, 2001), 511–12.

24. See John Worthen, *The Cambridge Introduction to Samuel Taylor Coleridge* (Cambridge: Cambridge University Press, 2010), 28.

Coleridge is indebted to a number of writers.[25] Coleridge claims to have written the poem in the summer of 1797, but there is good reason to think that he wrote it later than that. Not surprisingly, many critics find it impossible to believe that Coleridge could ever have remembered fifty-four lines from a "dream." Then there is the question of the "person from Porlock," who seems most likely to be a literary device. So, whatever we may think of the poem, the story behind its creation doesn't hold up.

A Little Help from My Friends

It is Friedrich Nietzsche (1844–1900) who insists that "life itself is *essentially* a process of appropriating. . . . 'Exploitation' does not belong to a corrupted or imperfect, primitive society: it belongs to the *essence* of being alive."[26] Certainly all art making is *essentially* appropriation. The *Oxford English Dictionary* defines "appropriation" as "taking as one's own or to one's own use."[27] A simple example of this is that poetry and novels rely upon "appropriating" words from some language. But improvising requires more than just borrowing from language. It requires appropriating from life, from the world of ideas, and from the "language" of painting or film or sculpture or dance. Indeed, it is so basic to artistic improvisation that the novelist Margaret Drabble (1939–) boldly admits that "appropriation is what novelists do. Whatever we write is, knowingly or unknowingly, a borrowing. Nothing comes from nowhere."[28] At least for human improvisers, we are constantly appropriating.

The question, then, is simply: How much does any given piece of art depend upon another? The answer is: it all depends. For appropriation and dependency represent a rather wide spectrum that has representatives all along the way. Even if one tries to come up with examples that are truly "original," one inevitably can find influences and sources for such examples. A typical example of an

25. Elisabeth Schneider, *Coleridge, Opium, and Kubla Khan* (New York: Octagon, 1983), 17.

26. Friedrich Nietzsche, *Beyond Good and Evil*, trans. Judith Norman (Cambridge: Cambridge University Press, 2002), §259.

27. *The Oxford English Dictionary*, 2nd ed., s.v. "appropriation."

28. Margaret Drabble, *The Red Queen: A Transcultural Tragicomedy* (Orlando: Harcourt, 2004), x.

"original" piece of art is Igor Stravinsky's (1882–1971) *The Rite of Spring* (*La Sacre du Printemps*), which first premiered in 1913. Consider the following description of it from 1927: "Harmonic tradition collapsed; everything became permissible and it was but necessary to find one's bearings in these riches obtained by this unexpected 'license'. . . . Stravinsky broke down everything old at one blow."[29] The musicologist and Stravinsky scholar Richard Taruskin quotes these words and then says the following:

> Minus the rampant animus, this is more or less how *The Rite of Spring* is still viewed today. The usual account of the work places almost exclusive emphasis on its putative rupture with tradition; and despite all his subsequent disclaimers, that is the view the composer chose to abet, increasingly alienated as he was from the cultural milieu in which the ballet was conceived. It was, however, precisely because *The Rite* was so profoundly *traditional*, both as to cultural outlook and as to musical technique, that Stravinsky was able to find through it a voice that would serve him through the next difficult phase of his career. Precisely because *The Rite* was neither rupture nor upheaval but a magnificent extension, it revealed to Stravinsky a path that would sustain him through a decade of unimaginable ruptures and upheavals brought on by events far beyond his control.[30]

Taruskin's point is that what *sounds* so new and different is actually very strongly grounded in the tradition of Russian music that Stravinsky inherits. *The Rite* is thus marked by its fusion of traditional and modern elements. And Taruskin points out that Stravinsky, although wavering back and forth, generally chose to promote the "revolutionary" interpretation of the piece, since that made *The Rite* (and thus Stravinsky himself) seem all the more remarkable. Yet this kind of rhetoric is often just that: ways of talking that make pieces of art seem more extraordinary than they really are by overemphasizing the "new" aspects and downplaying the more "traditional" ones. However "innovative" a piece of art might be, it is always still very strongly dependent upon tradition.

29. Leonid Sabaneyeff, *Modern Russian Composers*, trans. Judah A. Joffe (1927; repr., New York: Da Capo, 1975), 78–79. Quoted in Richard Taruskin, *Stravinsky and the Russian Traditions: A Biography of the Works through Mavra*, vol. 1 (Berkeley: University of California Press, 1996), 847.

30. Taruskin, *Stravinsky and the Russian Traditions*, 847.

The avant-garde composer Pierre Boulez (1925–) captures this quite nicely when he says:

> The composer is exactly like you, constantly on the horns of the same dilemma, caught in the same dialectic—the great models and an unknown future. He cannot take off into the unknown. When people tell me, "I am taking off into the unknown and ignoring the past," it is complete nonsense.[31]

Indeed, what *could* "taking off into the unknown" possibly look (or sound) like?

Improvisation with what is available to an artist can take many different forms. The painter and sculptor George Braque (1882–1963) began to experiment with making collages out of newspaper fragments, ticket stubs, pieces of wood, fabric, stamps, and other items. Here we have a kind of improvisation that takes the detritus of human life and makes it into something artistic. In turn, film directors often look to novels for their material. There are various versions of Jane Austen novels that attempt to be as "faithful" as possible to the original. The photographer Sherrie Levine (1947–) has made a career of photographing photographs of other photographers and then presenting the results as her own. She is known for an exhibition titled "After Edward Weston" (1980) in which she presented her photographs of Walker Evans's photographs.

Or, to offer another example, folk music likewise relies on borrowing and "remixing" strands from other pieces of music that can result in either something that is very close to an existing song or something quite different from anything that already exists. Folk music is so strongly "intertextual" that, if such borrowing ceased, so would the very genre. For this reason, the musicologist Charles Seeger writes, "The attempt to make sense out of copyright law reaches its limit in folk song. For here is the illustration par excellence of the Law of Plagiarism. The folk song is, by definition and, as far as we can tell, by reality, entirely a product of plagiarism."[32] As I mentioned earlier, rock music would be unthinkable without the very direct influence of the blues. It was not just that rock musicians

31. Pierre Boulez, *Orientations*, trans. Martin Cooper (Cambridge, MA: Harvard University Press, 1986), 454.
32. Charles Seeger, "Who Owns Folklore?—A Rejoinder," *Western Folklore* 21 (1962), 97.

were listening to blues musicians and getting ideas; it was that they were actually ripping them off. For example, Led Zeppelin's eponymous debut album is heavily indebted to Willie Dixon's songs "You Shook Me," "I Can't Quit You Baby," and "You Need Love." Of course, once such pieces of art start to generate huge revenues, creative borrowing becomes problematic. Thus, Dixon sued Led Zeppelin. The family of African composer Solomon Linda, who wrote the song "The Lion Sleeps Tonight" (used by Disney in *The Lion King*), filed suit against Abilene Music. Picasso and others appropriated from African art back when such borrowing seemed perfectly acceptable. More recently, Bob Dylan borrowed from the Confederate poet Henry Timrod. Dylan's "When the Deal Goes Down" has the line "more frailer than the flowers, these precious hours," whereas Timrod's "Rhapsody of a Southern Winter Night" goes, "A round of precious hours . . . And strove, with logic frailer than the flowers."

Perhaps we need to be more honest and simply recognize that borrowing is what makes art *possible*. Back in 1876, Ralph Waldo Emerson (1803–82) had already noted:

> Our debt to tradition through reading and conversation is so massive, our protest or private addition so rare and insignificant,—and that commonly on the ground of other reading or hearing,—that, in a large sense, one would say, there is no pure originality. All minds quote. Old and new make the warp and woof of every moment. There is no thread that is not a twist of these two strands. By necessity, by proclivity, and by delight, we all quote.[33]

Of course, there has long been something like a consensus on what *kind* of borrowing is permissible. The poet John Milton (1608–74) gives us the formula in brief: "For such a borrowing as this, if it be not bettered by the borrower, among good authors it is accounted Plagiare."[34] The composer Johann Mattheson (1681–1784) expands on this idea: "Borrowing is permissible; but one must return the thing borrowed with interest, i.e., one must so construct and develop

33. Ralph Waldo Emerson, "Quotation and Originality," in *The Collected Works of Ralph Waldo Emerson*, vol. 8, *Letters and Social Aims*, ed. Ronald A. Bosco, Glen M. Johnson, and Joel Myerson (Cambridge, MA: Belknap, 2010), 91.

34. John Milton, *Eikonoklastes*, in *Complete Prose Works of John Milton*, vol. 3, *1648–1649*, ed. Merritt Y. Hughes (New Haven: Yale University Press, 1962), 547.

imitations that they are prettier and better than the pieces from which they are derived."[35]

It shouldn't be difficult to see that defining the role of artists in terms of improvisation changes pretty much everything. If artists are indebted to one another, there can be no "lone" genius, disconnected from the community. Instead, we are all improvisers together, quoting one another, saying the same thing in different ways, and providing different perspectives. There is an ever-shifting balance between quotation and originality, between old and new, between you and me. Some of what I say is more "mine"; some is more "yours"; some is more "tradition." Getting the exact ownership right may only be possible to a certain extent. And then the question is: Does it really matter?

Copyright: The Artist and the Church

A few years ago I was preparing an article for an edited collection of papers that had been given at the Wheaton Theology Conference. I quoted eight lines from a Duke Ellington (1899–1974) song called "Come Sunday." And I ended up having to pay the publisher $50 for those eight lines (they originally wanted $75, but I countered with $35 and we compromised at $50). What makes this a particularly interesting story is that that chapter is filled with quotes from philosophers and theologians. Yet, *in every other case*, the copyright exemption known as "fair use" came into play. I was writing an academic essay using published work that was "factual" rather than fiction, and I was only using relatively short quotations. But "fair use" for songs, symphonies, poems, films, and novels is more complicated. Or, to put that slightly differently, anything that counts as an artistic product is generally protected against public performance—or even simple repetition. There *are* some exemptions. A notable one is the "religious service exemption," US Copyright Law section 110[3], which allows "performances of a dramatico-musical work of a religious nature, or display of a work, in the course of services at a place of worship." Then there is the exception for "performance of a nondramatic literary or musical

35. Johann Mattheson, *Johann Mattheson's* Der vollkommene Capellmeister, trans. Ernest Charles Harriss (Ann Arbor: UMI Research Press, 1981), 298.

work otherwise than in a transmission to the public, without any purpose of direct or indirect commercial advantage and without payment of any fee or other compensation for the performance to any of its performers, promoters, or organizers" (US Copyright Law section 110[4]), though that continues with a list of further qualifications. Then there is the "fair use" exemption (US Copyright Law section 107), which is vague, as well as various "educational" exemptions that are—taken all together—somewhat complicated.[36]

Thus, even though the books that I cited are copyrighted, Duke Ellington's song simply "stuck out" as something worthy of special attention. Being a great fan of Ellington, I'm glad his heirs are getting their due, and yet something seems wrong here. I was allowed to quote a whole paragraph (or more) from any of the other authors, but eight lines from Ellington suddenly meant I had to pay up. That raises a further question: How many things are actually copyrighted or trademarked that might seem to be common property? Every time I visit my local AMC theater, they play a clip that says, "Silence is Golden®." How can anyone trademark such a common saying? Were you aware that the folk song "Old King Cole" is owned by Cecil Sharp, who has made a profession out of "collecting" old folk songs and copyrighting them under his name (and then collecting the profits)?[37] Did you know that the words "old fashioned" are owned by the giant food conglomerate Mrs. Smith's?

One can only ask, where is all this to end? The editors of an anthology on copyright put forth what would seem to be the two obvious extremes. On the one hand, we might end up with "copyright totalitarianism" in which music and films and other forms of art or literature are so closely monitored that some central agency "knows" how long you are listening to a piece of music or reading a particular book (perhaps with a GPS loaded on your iPad or Kindle). You are charged a monthly usage fee and both fined and denied further access if you don't pay. Sampling and borrowing

36. For a thoughtful and enlightening discussion of fair use, see Patricia Aufderheide and Peter Jaszi, *Reclaiming Fair Use: How to Put Balance Back in Copyright* (Chicago: University of Chicago Press, 2011).

37. Georgina Boyes, *The Imagined Village: Culture, Ideology and the English Folk Revival* (Manchester: Manchester University Press, 1993), 224. Further, the 1956 Wihtol v. Wells case established that one could take a public domain folk melody, put new words to it, and then sue anyone else who put new words to it.

would become odd curiosities of the past, with future generations wondering how anyone could think to do anything so *outré*.[38] The alternative is what those same editors call "copyright anarchy," in which the music, book, and other such artistic industries realize that there is simply no way to control sampling, downloading, copying, and borrowing.

As should be clear, neither of these extremes is desirable. Artists, like any other laborers, are "worthy of their hire," and we should have respect for their improvised art. And yet, one cannot help but question aspects of copyright law. Above all, it is conceptually problematic, precisely because the idea that one can "own" a cultural product is a relatively new and ultimately questionable idea. Of course, it may seem obvious to us, but our ideas about copyright and the very idea of "ownership" of cultural/intellectual property *are 100 percent culturally dependent*. This is one reason why that annoying movie clip "You Wouldn't Steal a Purse" is conceptually problematic.[39] *We* have developed these ideas regarding ownership of cultural property, but they are relatively new ideas and quite foreign to the ways in which people have generally thought in the past.

Further, given what we have seen of the modern/romantic paradigm, it should come as no surprise that such a paradigm is the basis for much—if not all—of our thinking about copyright. Consider what two experts on copyright say: "Today's copyright law requires that somebody (or several somebodies) be the author(s) of a copyrighted work. There is no place for truly collective authorship based on notions of group work." Yet we have seen that we are *always* working together in some way. However, it turns out that the romantic paradigm has been very useful—*economically*—for many companies. "Music, publishing, and movie executives constantly

38. A landmark case that could spell such a future concerns rapper Biz Markie's sampling of twenty seconds of Gilbert O'Sullivan's "Alone Again (Naturally)" in the song "Alone Again" on his album *I Need a Haircut*. O'Sullivan successfully sued Markie and, with that ruling, sampling in rap has markedly decreased. The album *I Need a Haircut* (Cold Chilin' Records, 1991) is still available but without the offending song. For a fuller account of this story, see Siva Vaidhyanathan, *Copyrights and Copywrongs: The Rise of Intellectual Property and How It Threatens Creativity* (New York: New York University Press, 2001), 141–43. After the Biz Markie lawsuit, rappers who sample have needed to get permission to do so from the copyright holder.

39. An excellent response to this clip can be found at http://www.videosift.com /video/I-Wouldnt-Steal-A-Purse-But-I-Do-Download-Films.

invoke the genius-creator with piety, even when their own artists demonstrate the need and will to collaborate widely and even though their own businesses return relatively little to most creators. They put their celebrities out in front to celebrate the Romantic notion of the creator, while they depend on crude economic calculation to lay claim to works for hire."[40] "Works for hire" means that, if someone employs you to make art, then they own the finished project, which is why so many musicians (for instance) feel "used" by record companies.

Unfortunately, though, these ideas also have serious consequences for the flourishing of creativity. When Marc Gershwin, nephew of George and Ira, worries that "someone could turn 'Porgy and Bess' into rap music," we should worry about his worry.[41] Why *shouldn't* someone turn *Porgy and Bess* into rap music? Gershwin's worry is all the more worrisome when we remember that *Porgy and Bess* is the result of heavy borrowing from African American music (in some cases even "stealing" traditional songs). But, of course, Gershwin's music has been the source of so many improvisations by both black and white musicians that the borrowing has gone full circle. What is more problematic is that copyright laws have only gotten progressively more restrictive. We have moved from (1) the American Constitution's provision of fourteen years (with the possibility of an additional fourteen years, if the author was still alive) to (2) twenty-eight years with a renewal period of twenty-eight years (1909) to (3) the length of the author's life plus fifty years (1976) to (4) the author's life plus seventy years (1998), which was enacted to protect some key Disney characters.

And it should be pointed out that ASCAP and BMI—companies that enforce copyrights—are very good at making people pay up. Although copyright is widely disregarded in certain parts of the world, the goal of such enforcers is that everyone pays. If you hold a parade (even a nonprofit one in your small town), you have to pay for the music you use. Yoga instructors are required to pay for the music they play. I actually called up BMI's customer service and asked, "If I just start singing a song in the park, do I have to pay?" To which the quick answer was, "Yes, because it's a public

40. Aufderheide and Jaszi, *Reclaiming Fair Use*, 23.
41. Quoted in Steve Zeitlin, "Strangling Culture with a Copyright Law," *New York Times*, April 25, 1998.

performance." And when I answered, "But I'm not charging any money," the answer was, "It's still a public performance." So you are—at least according to BMI's customer service—breaking the law if you start singing a tune while walking down the street. Probably the most egregious instance of being overbearing was ASCAP's attempt to get thousands of summer camps—including, most famously, Girl Scout Camps—to pay up for singing songs around the campfire. ASCAP's John Lo Frumento claimed, "They buy paper, twine and glue for their crafts—they can pay for the music, too. We will sue them if necessary."[42] It never actually came to that, because ASCAP was forced to back down because of bad public relations (people don't like you when you say mean things about the Girl Scouts).

Exactly where we go from here is unclear. Many people writing on copyright law realize that the law as it currently stands is unworkable and will only impoverish creativity. Some suggest that copyright should last somewhere along the lines of ten or fifteen years, perhaps with some possibility for renewal.[43] That would move copyright in the direction of the much shorter trademark protection on prescription medication. Of course, Patricia Aufderheide and Peter Jaszi have made an excellent case that "fair use" can come into play in many situations. Yet navigating fair use is somewhat complicated. It would also recognize what seems to be the inevitable reality that makes sharing music, films, or whatever through the internet is increasingly easy.

But someone might ask: Why have you spent so much time talking about copyright in a book on the arts and the church? The answer is simple: because copyright laws all too strongly mirror the modern/romantic paradigm by assuming that works of art are discrete units of originality, when they are instead interconnected "pieces" of a much larger artistic fabric.[44] So the very notion of copyright and what it means to "create" a piece of art needs to be seriously

42. "ASCAP Faces the Music," *Austin American-Statesman*, September 1, 1996. Quoted in Kembrew McLeod, *Owning Culture: Authorship, Ownership, and Intellectual Property Law* (New York: Peter Lang, 2001), 55.

43. For instance, see Rufus Pollock, "Forever Minus a Day? Some Theory and Empirics of Optimal Copyright" (http://www.rufuspollock.org/economics/papers /optimal_copyright.pdf).

44. This is one reason why I prefer the term "piece of art" as opposed to "work of art," since the latter suggests something discrete and original.

rethought, since these two notions go so closely together. My own inclination is that copyright should be significantly shortened and less restrictive. Yet that only gets at one practical aspect. Much more important would be a serious discussion of what to make of the very notion of copyright in light of the fact that any of our "creating" is ultimately *improvising*. My hope here is to help provoke that discussion.

Yet here I want to turn to the question of what it means to live improvisationally.

Living Improvisationally

Although the idea that we are made in God's image—the *imago Dei*—has been used in many ways (some of them questionable), it seems clear that part of what it means to be creatures that bear the divine image is that we are likewise artisans. Yet what does that mean? The creation narrative depicts God as the artisan *par excellence*. J. Richard Middleton points out that "it is due precisely to God's exercise of royal power that there is a stable, dependable cosmic structure." What that means for *us* is that "humans are *like God* in exercising royal power on earth" and also that "the divine ruler *delegated* to humans a share in his rule of the earth."[45] The very process that God has set in motion is one in which we are to share. We are thus artisans in God's image, though in a significantly lesser sense than God is an artisan. If we hold to the account of God as creating out of nothing, then clearly we are starkly different from God, for we always create *out of something*. However, even if we say that God "improvises" upon the formless void, his artisanal power is so much *greater* than ours in *quantity*, and his creation is so much more *original* than ours in *quality*, that comparison must be thoroughly qualified.

Yet, as part of that reality—and made in the image of this original improviser—we take part in that improvisatory movement in all that we do. As beings inhabiting the flux, we find our lives constantly in motion. As creatures embedded in multiple and ever-changing historical and cultural milieus, our identities and very being arise

45. J. Richard Middleton, *The Liberating Image: The* Imago Dei *of Genesis 1* (Grand Rapids: Brazos, 2005), 81, 88.

from our relations to others and the world we inhabit. As improvisers, we constantly reshape that which is at hand rather than "create." We improvise with each sentence that comes from our mouths and with every action that we perform. Even though we have rituals for greeting and eating and worship, we are constantly improvising upon them.

How does all of this work out in our lives? If we are truly improvisational beings, then it would seem that *everything* we do is improvisation. We might simply say that we dwell in the world *improvisationally*. In all that we do, we are engaging in *creatio ex improvisatio*. Here we need to go back to the idea of a "beginning."

Earlier, I used the phrase "always already" in regard to the call and the response. Central to Martin Heidegger's early thought is the idea that *Dasein*—which is how he speaks of human existence—always finds itself *already* at home in the world, in the midst of language, and with tools ready at hand.[46] The phrase *immer schon* (always already) is like a *Leitmotiv* in *Being and Time*. And it plays a similar role in Chrétien. After citing Heidegger's claim that we are able to speak only because we have "always already [*toujours déjà*], listened to speech,"[47] Chrétien goes on to say, "We are entangled in speech as soon as we exist, before we have ever uttered a word, and in this sense we have always already listened and obeyed."[48] Such is true of speech, but we have seen that it is likewise true of the call (*l'appel*) in general. We have already seen that this call comes from God.

Yet this raises an interesting question: Are the calls of creation truly the first calls? Might there not be ones that preceded even them? The clue that raises at least the possibility of such a question comes in the portion of the Genesis narrative in which humankind is brought into being. In a dramatic departure from the previous refrain of "let there be," we find "let *us* make humankind in *our* image, according to *our* likeness" (Gen. 1:26, italics added). Whether

---

46. See Martin Heidegger, *Being and Time*, trans. John Macquarrie and Edward Robinson (New York: Harper & Row, 1962).

47. Here Chrétien is citing the French translation of Heidegger's *Unterwegs zur Sprache* (*Acheminement vers la parole*), trans. Jean Beaufret, Wolfgang Brockmeier, and François Fédier (Paris: Gallimard, 1976), 241. Interestingly enough, whereas the French *toujours déjà* would translate as "always already," Heidegger only uses *schon* (rather than *immer schon*) in this passage. However, the *immer* can be read as implied.

48. Jean-Louis Chrétien, *The Call and the Response*, trans. Anne A. Davenport (New York: Fordham University Press, 2004), 28.

the use here of "us" and "our" is itself truly an indication of the
Trinity is less important than the doctrine itself. For, if God is not
one but three, then there is reason to think that some sort—however it might be conceived—of "call" and "response" goes back
and forth between these three persons. Moreover, if God is eternal,
then it makes little sense to speak of a "first" call. The relationship
of the persons of the Trinity has been eloquently described by the
fourth century Eastern fathers Gregory of Nyssa and Basil the Great
with the term περιχώρησις (perichōrēsis, Lat. circum-incedere), from
which we get "circumincession," which means "to move around in."
Perichōrēsis is the divine dance of the persons of the Trinity in which
they move around, with, and in each other. But surely perichōrēsis
could likewise be thought of in terms of a call and response—not a
divine dance but a divine discourse of ceaseless calls and responses
reverberating and interpenetrating each other. And, should we read
the "let us" as simply God's speaking of the celestial hierarchy (a
common enough reading of this passage, even among Christians),
we also find evidence of calls that precede the calls of creation. John
speaks of the "four living creatures" in the heavenly realm who sing
"day and night without ceasing": "Holy, holy, holy, the Lord God the
Almighty, who was and is and is to come" (Rev. 4:8). This is truly a
continual call, a call that continues throughout eternity. Moreover,
John is echoing something already found in the Hebrew Bible: in
responding to Job, God says that "the morning stars sang together
and all the heavenly beings shouted for joy" (Job 38:7).

In either case, by the time the call reaches us, it is never the first
call. We are always already caught up in the improvisatory movement that makes language and life possible. To speak is to be part
of an ongoing conversation and also to be part of an ever-evolving
hybridity of others and self. As someone who speaks with many
voices, I am not simply my own voice but a polyphony of voices.
Thus, the I for Chrétien is no "self-contained" or "self-constituted"
I. Instead, it is composed of multiple voices.

To improvise is always to speak to others, with others (even when
one improvises alone), and in the name of others. For instance, if
I'm playing one of the perennial standards of jazz, I do so along
with so many others—whether those playing alongside me, or those
playing the tune in some other corner of the world, or all those who
have played it before. Jazz musicians typically have a sense of what
the author of Hebrews calls "so great a cloud of witnesses" (Heb.

12:1). Moreover, when I play a tune, I am never simply improvising on that tune alone. I am improvising on the tradition formed by the improvisations upon that tune—what literary theorists call its "reception history," or how a particular piece of literature or music has been received in history.

Whereas, in regard to literature, Harold Bloom has spoken of "the *anxiety* of influence"—which is the desire to be new, fresh, and original—jazz musicians would rather speak of "the *joy* of influence."[49] Bloom's talk of "anxiety" stems from the romantic paradigm of art, with its drive to be "original." The primary artistic goal in the modern/romantic paradigm is to carve out a place for oneself by overcoming the influence of previous artists. One wants to become (to use Bloom's language) a "strong poet" who stands out as unique and thus distances herself from the tradition. But jazz provides an entirely different model. As a jazz improviser, one becomes part of a community of improvisers. As improviser, one works with material that already exists rather than creating *ex nihilo*. As improviser, one is aware of being wholly indebted to the past. As improviser, one speaks in the name of others. As improviser, one joins a conversation.

Although Chrétien almost certainly did not have jazz in mind, he opens *The Call and the Response* with a quotation from Joseph Joubert that captures these aspects perfectly: "In order for a voice to be beautiful, it must have in it many voices together."[50] My voice is always composed of many voices and so is never simply "my own." When I speak, I am always speaking on behalf of others. My voice contains their voices. Or, as my doctoral advisor Rudolf Bernet beautifully puts it, "Somebody who must hold a lecture discovers that he or she is continually paraphrasing other authors and speaks as well in the name of colleagues and friends."[51] I have often thought of this quote as I give lectures, for I realize that I am speaking in the name of Bernet and so many others. What emerges in this improvisation upon improvisation is an ever-evolving hybridity in which identity and ownership are often stretched to their limits.

49. Harold Bloom, *The Anxiety of Influence* (Oxford: Oxford University Press, 1973), and John P. Murphy, "Jazz Improvisation: The Joy of Influence," *Black Perspective in Music* 18, no. 1/2 (1990): 7–19.

50. Chrétien, *Call and the Response*, 1.

51. Rudolf Bernet, "The Other in Myself," in *Deconstructive Subjectivities*, ed. Simon Critchley and Peter Dews (Albany: State University of New York Press, 1996), 177.

Is an improvisation "mine" if it is so indebted to other improvisers? And how is even my identity as an improviser connected with those of other improvisers?

To describe a community as one of multiple voices is indeed right. Yet perhaps it does not go quite far enough. In juxtaposition to (that is, *in addition to*) the notion of "polyphony," we need to set the notion of heterophony—both descriptively and prescriptively. First, whereas polyphony provides the aspect of a *multiplicity* of voices, heterophony emphasizes the *otherness* of those voices. If there is to be true otherness, then we cannot—and should not—have a beautifully blended polyphony. Indeed, one can argue that this lovely notion of polyphony is all too liberal and modern, for it wishes to smooth over the difficulties and the dissonance. Second, heterophony emphasizes the idea of differing voices that do not simply blend or produce a pleasing harmony but remain distinct and sometimes dissonant, sometimes precisely when we would rather they were not.[52] This is not to say that now dissonance takes center stage; rather, it is to say that dissonance—sometimes eventually resolved and sometimes not—is simply part of that conversation. Only if there is true heterophony can there be the expression and existence of otherness. Without such openness to such dissonance, we would not have the late Beethoven quartets. Harmony may *arrive*, but that arrival may well have to do with a change in *us* as listeners, and perhaps a revision of what counts as "harmony."[53]

Having considered how our lives are improvisational, let me close this chapter by considering how church communities are responding to the call to live improvisationally by promoting the arts and supporting artists. In working on this book, I've visited a wide variety of churches that are doing remarkable things. One church that particularly stands out—in many ways—is Saint Gregory of

---

52. David Cunningham rightly points out that "polyphony" and "harmony" are *not* synonymous, even though they are often taken to be such. Given that difference, he thinks the notion of polyphony is sufficient, since "polyphony could theoretically be either 'harmonious' or 'dissonant.'" Yet it is precisely because I want to emphasize the existence of (and *need for*) dissonance and difference that I think we need the notion of heterophony. See David S. Cunningham, *These Three Are One: The Practice of Trinitarian Theology* (Malden, MA: Blackwell, 1998), 128.

53. See my "Improvising Texts, Improvising Communities: Jazz, Heteronomy, and *Ekklēsia*," in *Resonant Witness*, ed. Jeremy S. Begbie and Steven Guthrie (Grand Rapids: Eerdmans, 2011).

Nyssa Episcopal Church in San Francisco. Saint Gregory of Nyssa is a church that works particularly hard to get *everyone* attending the worship service involved. When I spoke to Sanford Dole, the church's music director, after a service, he mentioned that a central goal is to achieve "shared leadership" in which the congregation has a strong sense of being involved. In an interview, Richard Fabian, one of the two founders of St. Gregory's, sounds this same theme: "St. Gregory's liturgy is deeply and radically traditional. This means shared leadership; real lay authority with lay liturgists, composers, preachers, and worship leaders. . . . It puts the invitation to participate in worship at the center. In a passive, consumerist culture, our congregation sings; people move from their pews, they touch each other."[54]

Now, this idea that participation is "radically traditional" may strike some readers as surprising. We often think of "traditional worship services" as ones in which the celebrant or pastor is the primary person of action. In such services, the congregation is often quite passive—occasionally they sing a hymn or song, but mostly they sit and listen. When Fabian speaks of "traditional," he means the *early church*, in which those attending were very much active participants. The Eucharist was an actual meal, and there was no elaborate hierarchy of clergy and laity. Simply put, these early services would have been highly interactive. And that is what St. Gregory's is attempting to regain. For instance, their *Music for Liturgy* (basically, their "hymnal" produced both by and for the church) has quite a number of pieces that are composed by various members of the church. In fact, the church has produced a CD with all original compositions. But that's not all: on its website, there is a large variety of liturgies and other resources for worship that can be used by any congregation. The church encourages visual artists by organizing a retreat for them twice a year, and it has a writers' group. *Everyone* in the church is encouraged to learn how to make icons, including children. The aim, says Sanford, is that they "feed off of each other's creative energy" in precisely the way I've talked about in this chapter.

Of course, there are many ways that the arts and artists receive support in various churches. Redeemer Presbyterian Church in New

54. See http://www.episcopalcafe.com/daily/sacraments/step_inside_st_gregory _of.php.

York City encourages its artistic members by getting them involved in worship services. Given that the church is located in Manhattan, there are plenty of professional artists from which to draw. Thus, professional instrumentalists and vocalists lead the congregation in a wide variety of musical expressions. The bulletin covers and other publications are the work of graphic and visual artists, while professional actors often read the Scripture readings. But Redeemer goes even further, for it offers what they term "vocation groups"—many different small groups specifically designed to provide fellowship for actors, classical music performers, composers, filmmakers, or jazz musicians.[55] Redeemer also organizes "faith and work seminars" designed for artists to gather to discuss how their belief affects their work as artists, as well as philosophical and theological questions that arise in their daily work. The church holds evening "open forums" that employ a combination of music, lectures by Timothy Keller (the church's main pastor), and public discussion. Naturally, few churches have the opportunity to employ and support such a wide range of talented professionals. On the other hand, in churches without so many professionals, there is far more opportunity for nonprofessionals to exercise and develop their own talents.

Saint Gregory the Great Church in Chicago (a Roman Catholic parish) has an "artists in residence" program. While many colleges or organizations have such programs, Saint Gregory the Great's is somewhat different. Consider how they explain it on the church's website: "The St. Gregory the Great outreach does not merely celebrate the efforts and talents of the individual artist, but melds those efforts and talents into a wider spiritual vision and mission. We describe this wider spiritual vision and mission as 'Evangelization Through the Arts.'" The goal, then, is twofold: the church seeks to support artists who can "make the parish a base where their art can not only be created, but also shared with the community as a living expression of gospel faith and virtue." Artists truly become part of the community, for they are both supported and in turn "serve the parish mission in various practical ways."[56] Such two-way support is really the ideal for the church community.

Then there are the conferences put on by such megachurches as Willow Creek Community Church in South Barrington (in the

---

55. Of course, Redeemer also has groups for business people and educators.
56. See http://stgregory.net/index.php?page=artists-in-residence.

Chicago area) and Saddleback Church (in southern California). Having attended Saddleback's conference, I was impressed with the great variety of workshops being taught. For instance, one could sit in on a seminar with Jimmy and Carol Owens (two of the pioneers of contemporary Christian music) on the basics of songwriting. In private conversation with Jimmy Owens, I found him quite sensitive to the dangers to which Christian musicians are prone, such as making worship leading into a "performance," a common criticism of contemporary Christian musicians. But there were also workshops on topics such as "Creating a Culture of Worshipers," creating a dance ministry, and even the problem of "copyright compliance." Both Willow Creek and Saddleback have been exemplary in involving artistically talented individuals in their services. Both have worked hard to support artists of all types, these worship conferences being only one example.

Having considered improvisation as a new way of conceiving life and what we as artists do, we need to turn to some potential dangers.

4

On Not Being
an Artistic Whore

"Work is what you do for others, Liebchen, art is what you do for yourself." That quote comes from the servant of the artistic patron of Georges Seurat, painter of "Sunday at the Grand Jatte."[1] From the servant's point of view, his own work is something he does for other people. In contrast, the painting that he observes Seurat working on each Sunday is purely for Georges himself. We have already seen that this is a fairly common view about art. And surely there is something right about improvising for oneself—that one does so for one's own pleasure and the expression of one's thoughts and feelings. But, having said that, is that enough? If art is really only something one does for oneself, then it is rather solipsistic in nature—which is to say it is purely about oneself. I have certainly known artists—for instance, some of my own students—who claim that they enjoy performing music or painting just for themselves. I can't see anything wrong with that. Yet, in my experience, few artists make artistic things *only* for themselves. Normally, artists want others to share and appreciate their art, which means they are not making art *simply* for themselves. But this raises a number of questions. First, for whom should we be making art? Second, how

1. Stephen Sondheim, *Sunday in the Park with George* (New York: Revelation and Ritling, 1984), 74–75.

does what artists do relate to the community at large? Third, are there certain kinds of art that are "better" than others?

While these questions might at first seem to be important only for those who are artists in the more specialized sense of the term, they are questions that face all of us. If we are living works of art, then for whom are we fashioning our lives? One immediate answer is: God. Without doubt, all that we do is for God, to whom we owe our very beings. Yet the answer is inevitably more complicated than that, for all of us are part of communities—such as the communities of family, friends, church, and much more. Indeed, it is safe to say that one complication regarding the question of "for whom" is that we are all part of *multiple* communities, and satisfying all members in every community of which we're a part may not even be possible.

In any case, these questions bring us back to the dilemmas facing Asher Lev, who is forced to choose which community he will ultimately be loyal to.

The Story of Asher Lev

Whenever I teach my Philosophy of the Arts course at Wheaton College, I have students read Chaim Potok's book *My Name Is Asher Lev*. It's perfectly appropriate for Wheaton students because—like Asher—they face somewhat similar (even if not identical) sorts of questions and barriers. In chapter 2, we noted the warning that Asher receives from his mentor, Jacob Kahn, about art being like a religion, one greatly at odds with his and Asher's own Judaism. But here it is helpful to take a closer look at Asher's situation.

As a Hasidic Jew who wants to paint, Asher is deeply at odds with his religious tradition, his very conservative father (Aryeh), and his relatively passive mother (Rivkeh). Neither Aryeh nor Rivkeh can figure out what to do with their precocious son, who is clearly (as Asher himself puts it) "born with a gift," and starts to draw by age four.[2] Yet this supposed "gift" is clearly at odds with the expectations of Hasidic Judaism, in which painting simply isn't allowed. Naturally, this raises the question of exactly *where* this gift comes from: Is it from God or is it instead from the "sitra achra"

2. Chaim Potok, *My Name Is Asher Lev* (New York: Anchor, 2003), 5. Further citations from this text will be given by way of page numbers in parentheses.

(the Other Side)? But, even worse, Asher draws "twisted shapes, swirling forms," rather than images of comfort. "You should draw pretty things, Asher," says his mother Rivkeh. "You should make the world pretty, Asher. Make it sweet and pretty. It's nice to live in a pretty world" (17–18). But Asher does not want to draw pretty things or to make the world pretty. As he puts it (when his mother raises the question once again), "I don't like the world, Mama. It's not pretty. I won't draw it pretty" (28). And this determination *not* to draw the world pretty is only further strengthened as he learns of the deaths of millions of fellow Jews under the hands of Hitler and Stalin.

At the urging of his father Aryeh, who thinks that art is from the sitra achra, Asher briefly gives up art. Yet Asher's penchant and talent for drawing keep coming out in doodles in his school notebooks. Eventually, recognizing that Asher clearly has a gift, the Rebbe allows Asher to study with a Jewish artist named Jacob Kahn, who expressly identifies himself as "not . . . a Torah Jew . . . not a religious Jew" (194). Aryeh responds with a deep sense of pain, though Rivkeh is more equivocal in her reaction. Asher says to his father, "I don't want there to be trouble between us, Papa." To which Aryeh responds, "Asher, I know you don't want trouble. I am not accusing you, God forbid, of being an evil person. But there is something inside you I don't understand. It will bring trouble" (196).

Jacob Kahn introduces Asher to a new world and a new community—but not before warning him. He asks Asher, "Do you have any idea at all what you are getting into?" Asher replies (quite rightly and innocently), "No." And Jacob responds, "Become a carpenter. Become a shoemaker" (193). In other words, try something safe; do something that won't upset your parents and your religious community. But Asher wants to pursue his art, so Jacob tells him to study Picasso's *Guernica* and then asks him to read about the slaughter of the innocents in Matt. 2:16. Thus, to become an artist, Asher is forced to take on a new identity and distance himself from his own Hasidic community. Asher is also introduced to a book titled *The Art Spirit*, in which he reads that

> [the artist] should be careful of the influence of those with whom he consorts, and he runs a great risk in becoming a member of a large society, for large bodies tend toward the leveling of individuality to a common consent, the forming and adherence to a creed. (202)

He also reads that

> every great artist is a man who has freed himself from his family,
> his nation, his race. Every man who has shown the world the way to
> beauty, to true culture, has been a rebel, a "universal" without pa-
> triotism, without home, who has found his people everywhere. (203)[3]

Interestingly enough, after reading these passages, Asher says to
his mother, "I don't think I want to free myself in that way." And
she responds, "In what way do you want to free yourself, Asher?"
Asher can only say, "I don't know" (203–4). However, Asher soon
discovers that, in order to join the art world, he doesn't really have
a choice. It is quite telling that Jacob Kahn introduces Asher to
his friend Anna Schaeffer—a gallery owner who will become the
purveyor of Asher's art—as follows: "Anna, this is *my* Asher Lev.
Asher Lev, this is *my* Anna Schaeffer" (207, italics added). There
is a new sense of belonging, but one deeply at odds with the sense
of belonging to the community of Hasidic Jews. When Asher says
that he believes that "it is man's task to make life holy," Anna responds by saying, "Asher Lev, you are entering the wrong world."
"This world will destroy you," she adds, for "art is not for people
who want to make the world holy" (209–10). The choice that faces
Asher is made even more explicit when Jacob says the following
(which we noted at the beginning of chapter 2):

> You are entering a religion called painting. It has its fanatics and its
> rebels. And I will force you to master it. Do you hear me? . . . Asher
> Lev, it is a tradition of goyim and pagans. Its values are goyish and
> pagan. . . . Its way of life is goyish and pagan. In the entire history
> of European art, there has not been a single religious Jew who was
> a great painter. Think carefully of what you are doing before you
> make your decision. (213)

One might expect Asher to make an explicit choice at this point,
by making some kind of decisive gesture of embracing of this new
"religion" and turning his back on Hasidic Judaism. But Asher's

---

3. These quotations (and the page numbers cited) are taken from *My Name Is Asher
Lev*, but they are originally from Robert Henri, *The Art Spirit* (New York: Basic, 2007),
82 and 144. Not surprisingly, Henri is really just articulating a view of the artist based
on the modern/romantic paradigm.

choice is never so decisive as that. It is, as with many of our momentous choices, one made over the course of time, often by way of small choices and gestures, a choice made by continuing down a path rather than by undergoing some dramatic experience. Asher never fully embraces this new religion, but he embraces it enough that the Hasidic community eventually no longer knows what to make of him. The two religions are set on a collision course. After some time of study with Jacob Kahn, the Rebbe meets with Asher to warn him. "You are entering the world of the Other Side," he says. "Be careful of the Other Side, Asher Lev" (244). But, even though Asher does enter the world of the Other Side, he still attempts to keep one foot in the Hasidic community. The problem, though, is that the choice—at least as set up by Jacob Kahn—is a stark one. Jacob tells Asher, "You have a gift, Asher Lev. You have a responsibility. . . . Do you know what that responsibility is?" When Asher responds by saying that his responsibility is "to my people," Jacob tells him otherwise: "Listen to me, Asher Lev. As an artist, you are responsible to no one and to nothing, except to yourself and to the truth as you see it. Do you understand? An artist is responsible to his art. Anything else is propaganda" (217–18). There is a responsibility to truth, though it is truth as one sees it or defines it. Or, better yet, it is truth as one *feels* it. As Jacob puts it:

> The world is a terrible place. I do not sculpt and paint to make the world sacred. I sculpt and paint to give permanence to my feelings about how terrible this world truly is. Nothing is real to me except my own feelings . . . as I see them all around me in my sculptures and paintings. I know these feelings are true. (226)

A particularly poignant piece of advice that Jacob gives to Asher is that he avoid becoming a whore. At one point in the story, Jacob and Asher meet an artist who starts talking to them about what the latest trends are in art and how the art world (read: "money") is moving to Tokyo (and that he plans to move along with it). Once he's gone, Jacob refers to the man as a "whore"—someone who is willing to do whatever the art market demands. Jacob then says to Asher, "Do not become a whore" (256). When Asher protests that he has no such intentions, Jacob accuses him of already acting like a whore by putting his payos (i.e., his long hair curls) behind his ears to hide them.

Asher Lev, an artist who deceives himself is a fraud and a whore. You did that because you were ashamed. You did that because wearing payos did not fit your idea of an artist. Asher Lev, an artist is a person first. He is an individual. . . . Great artists will not give a damn about your payos; they will only give a damn about your art. (257)

Asher does eventually become a great artist, notorious for his *Brooklyn Crucifixion*, in which his mother is depicted upon a cross in her housedress. Just imagine how offensive a crucifixion scene—featuring his *mother*—would have been to an orthodox Jew. Even before showing this piece (and another crucifixion), Asher expresses his worry that he will hurt people (his family, his community) by allowing these works to be seen. To this worry, Anna (the gallery owner) responds that he should "forget for now about hurting people. Indulge your Jewish sentimentality when you return to Brooklyn" (345). Earlier, Jacob had told him, "Become a great artist. That is the only way to justify what you are doing to everyone's life" (278). But the Rebbe has another answer:

I do not hold with those who believe that all painting and sculpture is from the sitra achra. I believe such gifts are from the Master of the Universe. But they have to be used wisely, Asher. What you have done has caused harm. People are angry. They ask questions, and I have no answer to give them that they will understand. Your naked women were a great difficulty for me, Asher. But this is an impossibility. . . . I will ask you not to continue living here, Asher Lev. I will ask you to go away. . . . You are too close here to people you love. You are hurting them and making them angry. They are good people. They do not understand you. It is not good for you to remain here. . . . You have crossed a boundary. I cannot help you. You are alone now. I give you my blessings. (366–67)

And so Asher heads off to Europe, at home in neither his new religion nor his old.

Art and Christianity

Asher's story raises far more questions than we can possibly answer here. But it does provide a poignant account of some of the difficulties that any observant Jew would face as an artist. While there are significant differences between the expectations of the Hasidic community and the Christian community in regard to art, there are a number of problems that the two communities have very much in common. I do not intend to "solve" these problems here. Rather, I want to consider ways the artist can live in the tension that is inevitably part of the artist's position in a Christian community. Asher's father warns him that his artistic proclivities will only result in "trouble." Such is often the case with artists in religious communities—they stir up what some perceive as "trouble." However, rather than simply wishing to be *rid* of that tension, I think that it can become quite productive, depending on what one does with it. Indeed, it strikes me that artists and prophets often stir up the same kind of tension, for they often present pictures of us that are not comfortable. In short, I want to suggest that, as Christian artists, we can be like prophets: speaking the truth, even when it is neither convenient nor welcome.

Even though most versions of Christianity differ rather sharply from Hasidic Judaism regarding images, the history of Christianity and art has been somewhat difficult, to say the least. Of course, this tension between art and Christianity is rather hard to believe if one visits one of the great museums in the Western world: whether it's the Metropolitan Museum in Manhattan or the Tate Gallery in London or the Louvre in Paris, one finds gallery after gallery of distinctly *Christian* works of art. Moreover, many of these pieces were originally triptychs adorning an altar in a church or enjoying pride of place in a side chapel. It might seem that the church has always been at home with art.

While it is true that some of the earliest Christian art adorns the catacombs in Rome, there were early reservations—particularly stemming from Jewish prohibitions against images—about depictions of deity. Christianity has had fierce debates between the iconodules (those supporting icons) and iconoclasts (those against them), particularly in the fourth to eighth centuries. But that was not the end of such debates: the facade of Lincoln Cathedral in England—with its many statues missing heads and hands—provides a rather stark reminder that, during the sixteenth and seventeenth centuries, the iconoclasts were alive and well. Further, instrumental music has been a problem for some. Around AD 190, Clement of Alexandria wrote the following:

Leave the pipe to the shepherd, the flute to the men who are in fear of gods and intent on their idol-worshipping. Such musical instruments must be excluded from our wingless feasts. . . . But as for us, we make use of one instrument alone: only the Word of peace by whom we pay homage to God, no longer with ancient harp or trumpet or drum or flute which those trained for war employ.[4]

About two hundred years later, Chrysostom wrote something similar: "There is no need for the cithara, or for stretched strings, or for the plectrum and technique, or for any instrument; but, if you like, you may yourself become a cithara, mortifying the members of the flesh and making a full harmony of mind and body."[5] The idea here is that there is something "pure" about using the voice alone. Such arguments have been used by Eastern Orthodox theologians to keep Orthodox worship free from instruments for two millennia. Of course, even without instruments (or perhaps one might argue that precisely *because of that lack*), Orthodox churches have produced glorious music, not to mention stunning icons, making for an extremely rich artistic heritage.

In the Western world, when Christianity became the official religion of the Roman Empire, Christian art—architecture, painting, sculpture—naturally flourished. And it flourished throughout the medieval era, the Renaissance, and the early modern period. However, as art became a kind of substitute for religion (something we noted in chapter 2), religious art was increasingly marginalized. That brings us to our contemporary situation. The title of James Elkins's book *On the Strange Place of Religion in Contemporary Art* gets at the difficulty of introducing religion into the art world. Elkins admits that "once upon a time—but really, in every place and in every time—art was religious."[6] He further admits that art's inherent religiosity goes back through civilizations in Europe, Asia, and Africa, even back to the Neolithic period. So the fact that religion and art don't mix particularly well in our era is a very recent and unprecedented development. To begin to get at the extent of

4. Clement of Alexandria, *Christ the Educator*, Fathers of the Church (Washington, DC: Catholic University of America Press, 1954), 130.

5. John Chrysostom, "Exposition of Psalm 41," in *Source Readings in Music History*, rev. ed., ed. Oliver Strunk and Leo Treitler (New York: Norton, 1998), 125–26.

6. James Elkins, *On the Strange Place of Religion in Contemporary Art* (New York: Routledge, 2004), 5.

the problem, we can note that an exhibition of what I would take to be relatively sophisticated and thoughtful religious art, titled "The Next Generation: Contemporary Expressions of Faith," did get a showing in New York City, arguably the capital of the art world.[7] But it didn't make it into the Metropolitan Museum or the Guggenheim or any of the other major museums. Instead, it was shown at the Museum of Biblical Art housed in the American Bible Society. Further, the show didn't exactly get a rave review from the *New York Times*. Of course, the reviewer Ken Johnson admits that there is an inherent bias in the way the art world views art.

> Given our habits of viewing art aesthetically and psychologically rather than religiously, paintings that involve the appropriation of Christian imagery from antique pictures do not necessarily read as expressions of faith. . . . That most of the works in the show are bound up in outdated, illustrative and technical clichés should not necessarily be taken as an indictment of Christian faith as an artistic motivation.

He closes by writing the following: "So while most of the show's works stay well within the boundaries of the familiar and the conventional, the best ones show that Christian faith and artistic ambition can still be a combustible mixture."[8]

Consider what is being said here. First, he openly admits that the art world doesn't read things "religiously." Indeed, that's not one of its categories. So trying to bring something that is expressly religious into the art world is very difficult, since the art world does not have the proper interpretive grid to make sense of religious art. Second, artistically the pieces are considered to be "outdated." Here, of course, the demand for originality or innovation in the modern/romantic paradigm comes through very clearly. The paintings just aren't innovative enough. Of course, this is a common criticism of Christian art (and often made *within* the Christian world), whether Christian artists make "high art" or contemporary Christian music. One might be tempted simply to assume he is right, though one would need to see the works exhibited in order to decide. However, if we put these criticisms together with Elkins's comments on the

7. The catalog is Patricia C. Pongracz and Wayne Roosa, eds., *The Next Generation: Contemporary Expressions of Faith* (Grand Rapids: Eerdmans, 2005).

8. Ken Johnson, "New Artists Who Are Motivated by Christianity," *New York Times*, August 19, 2005.

conditions for religious art to enter the contemporary discourse of art, we start to get an idea of just where things stand. Given that art was once religious, when did the problem of religion entering art begin? Elkins pinpoints it to sometime during the Renaissance, when "it became possible to make visual objects that glorified the artist and even provoked viewers to think more of the artist's skills than the subject of the artwork."[9] There is clearly a tension here: at least historically, artworks done by Christians were primarily designed to glorify *God*. That the artist would now get top billing just doesn't fit with the historic expectations of art created within the context of the church. Elkins readily admits that this claim could be and has been debated, which means that this story of the rupture of art and religion is neither neat nor clean. I think it's safe to say that making art—somewhere between the Renaissance and romanticism—became such that it was less about the *object* depicted than about the *subject* depicting it. In other words, art became more about the artist—the artist's own "vision" and the ideal of "expressing oneself." These may be rather tired buzzwords (worthy of being put out to pasture), but they are still part of many artists' vocabularies, even in the twenty-first century.

Even though religious themes arise in modern art, Elkins notes that they have been decreasingly dealt with in a piously religious way. This is all the more true today, for religion usually only makes its way into fine art when it is treated nonreligiously. Elkins gives us two lists of qualifiers for what kind of religious art may be allowed in the art world. His first list is that such work is marked by "criticism, ironic distance, or scandal." His second list is rather similar: "irony, ambiguity, and uncertainty."[10] An example that Elkins gives of someone who simply doesn't "get" this is that of a student named Kim, who paints a huge hand reaching from heaven down to countless figures reaching back in prayer. It's sweet, sentimental, and hardly ironic. As Elkins responds (though not aloud) to Kim's question as to why you can't create "art that is really obviously religious" in the contemporary art world:

From Kim's point of view, ideas like complexity, ambiguity, difficulty, the absence of religion, and lack of sentiment were just the ideas of

9. Elkins, *On the Strange Place*, 7.
10. Ibid., 15, 48.

Western art criticism and it should be possible to make first-rate art that is both religious and optimistic. I could not find the words to tell her that complexity and the rest *are* postmodernism, that they *are* contemporary art.

"Modernism is just like that." It was all I could manage.[11]

While I think Elkins here needs a clearer distinction between modernity and postmodernity, there can be no arguing with the idea that modernity—whatever else it is—has no room for a nonambiguous, sentimental, optimistic religiosity. That's true in painting, and it is true in modern thought in general. One reason is that modernity problematizes religion and places it back into the private sphere. Perhaps one can paint such sentimental pictures *at home*, but they cannot be displayed in the usual institutions of the art world.

Yet this raises a further question: While we can all recognize the use of religious imagery by Andy Warhol as ironic or Anselm Kiefer as ambiguous, what about "true believers" who produce art that is, at turns, ironic, ambiguous, uncertain, and complex? In other words, it's not hard to see why Kim's painting would hardly get a viewing in the art world. Yet it's not immediately clear why truly religious artists who provide us with art that actually turns out to be ambiguous and complex are, as far as I can see, not being given a particularly warm reception by the art world. Of course, there are important exceptions—artists who have "made it" in the art world. Tim Hawkinson, who has a number of commissioned paintings in the Getty Museum in LA, has had his work *Pentecost* installed in the Ace Gallery (Los Angeles). The piece is oblique, but it's clearly religious—and, given where it was located, I think we can say that it has been accepted into the art world. One can also name other artists with strong religious commitments who have been recognized by the art world, such as Tim Rollins or Makoto Fujimura, a member of the council of the National Endowment for the Arts. Again, though, these are exceptions.

To make my point, let me provide an example. Bruce Herman (1953–), someone whom I consider a gifted and serious artist, tells the following story:

> I showed my Golgotha paintings (a series of overtly religious images based upon the Passion/Stations of the Cross) to a museum curator

11. Ibid., 31.

[Carl Belz at the Rose Art Museum at Brandeis University] who had formerly expressed interest in my work and who had included me in an exhibit at his museum. When he saw the Passion paintings, he wrote to me saying that he thought I might have either lost my mind or gone off the deep end with religion. "Nobody believes this crap anymore Herman—you can't make religious paintings these days. You're a very strong painter, but your subject matter is anachronistic and frankly untenable." I told him I hoped he lived long enough to eat his words.[12]

Herman tells me he's grateful to Belz for being honest enough to explain why he rejected his work and making it clear that it was *not* for artistic reasons. As Herman puts it: "Most of the time I've gotten the polite but dishonest brush off." Perhaps it is that these works are not ironic, ambiguous, or uncertain *enough*—that their irony is too gentle or their ambiguity is still too unambiguous. Yet I suspect (though I admit I cannot prove) that it comes down to something more like the following: in the art world, you can present religious themes so long as you don't actually *believe* in them. If one catches a whiff of genuine belief, your work may no longer pass muster.

But why is such art excluded? I think the only possible answer is that such a requirement is the result of sheer *dogmatism*, one that actually mimics what we find in certain religious expressions. The insistence on these characteristics is (to use the phrase that Elkins uses) a result of "the faith of the art world."[13] I think the real reason that art is separated from religion is that the art world is *all too like* religion, not here in the sense of having "replaced" religion or serving the same sociological function (though, as we have seen, this is probably true as well, at least to some extent), but in the sense of holding basic beliefs (basically, the art world's own kind of piety) that it sees no need to justify and that, outside the art world, may seem just as arbitrary as anything held by religious believers.

Thus, the real problem here is not that religion and art are so *different* but that they are so *alike*. Each of them has their respective "faiths." Given Foucault's idea of a discourse, we can say that each of these discourses has its priests, sacred texts, temples of worship, and rituals. And each set of practices is only "justified" *within* their

12. From an email exchange with Bruce Herman, October 12, 2007.
13. Elkins, *On the Strange Place*, 48.

respective discourses, not by something that we can call "objective reason." So, having asked the how and the why questions, let me venture into something much more speculative: the conditions under which it might be possible for religion to find a place in the art world. Or, how there might be a meeting of the minds, so to speak, between the church and the art world. Here I am thinking about the possibility of a genuine exchange: truly religious art not only getting its foot in the door of the art world but getting truly appreciated; and the church moving from its tendency toward "ghettoization," in which there is "religious art" and "serious art" and never the twain shall meet.

Here I think telling the story of philosophy is extraordinarily instructive. Not so very long ago, the presence of religious folk in professional philosophical circles was virtually unthinkable in the United States. Part of this was because philosophy in this country was largely dominated by logical positivism—a view that held that all religious, ethical, and aesthetic claims did not even qualify as "statements" or "propositions." They were, so the logical positivists insisted, simply expressions of emotion.[14] Thus, even the seemingly meaningful statement "rape is wrong" simply means "I don't like rape." Now, eventually, logical positivism came to an end because people finally realized that its basic tenet—"accept only that which is analytically true or empirically justifiable"—is *itself* neither analytically true nor empirically justifiable. In other words, that very tenet is simply dogmatism, even though the logical positivists saw themselves as hyperrational and the apotheosis of high modernity. But, then, with logical positivism exposed as just another kind of dogmatism, a strange thing happened. Religious—particularly Christian—philosophers started to argue that, given that *all* philosophical systems have their respective dogmatic elements that they accept by faith, Christian philosophy was in no way inferior to any other kind of philosophy. Contrary to Elkins's use of the term "postmodernism" (in which, according to Elkins, "postmodern art has only made the break [from religion] more decisive"),[15] it is actually postmodernity—at least of the philosophical variety—that

14. In case you're thinking that this sounds vaguely like what the authors of *The Green Book* were saying, you're right. Logical positivism naturally leads to aesthetic relativism (or what they would have called "aesthetic emotivism").
15. Elkins, *On the Strange Place*, 12.

has made the entrance of religion into philosophy possible. For, under the tight rule of modernity, anything that didn't meet the criteria of a rather rigid version of "reason" simply wasn't taken seriously. Yet, if postmodern thinkers have shown us anything, it is that there is always something like "faith" at the heart of what we call "reason." This is a claim that philosopher Jacques Derrida has made as forcefully as any.[16] Of course, once we recognize this, then the hegemony of science (or, for that matter, philosophy) is put into serious question. This certainly does not mean that, now, everything is equally valid—or equally invalid. But it does alter the rules of the game. No longer can religion be rejected simply because it is based on "faith." While certain things may be more "objective" than others, every belief system is laden with something that we could call "faith"—something that functions as a basic presupposition or set of presuppositions.

And that leads us back to the impasse facing religion and art. Both of them have their "faiths." On the one hand, art would seem to be certain of its insistence that "real" art be uncertain, ironic, and ambiguous. Religion, on the other hand, would seem to insist on its clarion certainty and absolute truth. It seems rather strange that art would be so *certain* about its commitment to *uncertainty*. Perhaps, just like logical positivism, art needs to see whether its requirement can truly pass its own test. Is the art world capable of expanding its ambiguity and uncertainty to include *itself*? Just as radically, perhaps those who profess religious belief might be capable of admitting that their beliefs are not without at least some degree of ambiguity, uncertainty, and even paradox. Certainly the Christian artists I know hardly think that because one believes, all uncertainties or ambiguities simply disappear into thin air. Anyone who really understands the mystery of faith realizes that, in some ways, it is even more of a commitment to mystery than either agnosticism or atheism.

If Foucault is right that discourses are never static and so always capable of change, then it might just be possible to envision an art world in which religion receives a warmer—even if somewhat cautious—welcome, and a religious world in which art is appreciated

16. Jacques Derrida, "Faith and Knowledge: The Two Sources of 'Religion' at the Limits of Reason Alone," in *Acts of Religion*, ed. Gil Anidjar (New York: Routledge, 2002).

and taken seriously, again even if somewhat cautiously. After all, stranger things have happened. And it seems like they are already beginning to happen. The artist Theodore Prescott (1944–) has recently noted:

> I believe that the actual gap between the two subcultures [the art world and the church] is narrowing, with changes taking place in both. Today there are many more Christians active in the visual arts than twenty years ago, and it is no longer unusual to find churches that have started to use the arts for worship, outreach, or simple enjoyment. In the art world, postmodernism's critique of the monolithic and totalizing claims of modernity has sometimes had the effect of allowing religiously grounded belief a place at the table. And for about a decade the art world has had an interest in spirituality, which obviously has resonance with Christian belief and practice. It is encouraging to see a narrowing of the gap. Nevertheless, the division is still substantial.[17]

So there are reasons for cautious optimism. I find it heartening to think that such important (and well-accepted) composers as Olivier Messiaen (1908–92), Henryk Górecki (1933–2010), Arvo Pärt (1935–), and John Tavener (1944–) are Christians and that their work strongly attests to their religious belief. Perhaps the music world is a little more welcoming than the art world in general. Still, as should be clear, many of the assumptions and values of the art world simply aren't compatible with those of the church. Some of those differences have already been explored; others will be considered shortly. There is good reason, then, that Christian artists will feel a certain discomfort in being part of the art world, a kind of discomfort similar to the discomfort that Christians *should* feel in living in the world.

On Being an Artistic Whore

If Jacob Kahn is right, the greatest danger that Asher faces is that of becoming a whore. The specific instance that Jacob points out is that of Asher trying to hide his payos—the sign of his Jewishness.

17. Theodore Prescott, "Identity," in *It Was Good: Making to the Glory of God*, ed. Ned Bustard, 2nd ed. (Baltimore: Square Halo, 2006), 308.

Jacob's worry is that Asher might be too eager to please the art world. But note that there is the possibility of a dual "whoredom" at work here.

On the one hand, the artist might try to please the amorphous entity of "the art world"—which is, basically, composed of gallery owners, museum curators, critics, and a relatively small band of "culturati." In chapter 2, we noted Tom Wolfe's estimates that there are approximately ten thousand people composing what he calls "Cultureburg." Often, when artists speak of "selling out," they have in mind art that appeals to the masses. But Kahn rightly points out that one can be a whore to the art world. That point should not be lost on artists who are trying to retain their Christianity while appeasing the gods of art. The danger that Asher faces is that, in trying to appeal to the culturati, he jeopardizes his commitment to his own Hasidic community. One can argue, of course, that he has already compromised himself simply by becoming an artist, but hiding his payos is another sign of this compromise—and a particularly important one for a Hasidic Jew. So the problem is not *simply* one-sided. One can become a whore in more than one way. And, again, this is hardly a problem only for an artist like Asher Lev. We are all capable of compromising ourselves in small and large ways in order to gain the approval of others.

So how *does* one keep from becoming a whore? This question vexes many artists, but it becomes doubly problematic for the Christian artist. Some Christians in the arts "solve" the problem by seeing themselves as Christians who also happen to be artists (or, sometimes, the other way around).[18] Yet a simple semantic change hardly fixes the problem. If Jacob Kahn is right that "painting"—or simply art—is itself a religion (or at least has certain requirements of its members that may be at odds with the requirements of religions such as Christianity), then the problem may be one of two religions competing with each other. While one might be tempted to say that Kahn's claim is too strong, art during modernity has generally functioned as something akin to religion, a point that we noted in detail in chapter 2. With the decline of Christianity at the end of the eighteenth century and the beginning of the nineteenth century, many saw religion as being replaceable by art. Certainly it has come to occupy a place in our society that is remarkably *like*

18. Christian philosophers sometimes take the same tack.

a religion, in certain respects. Wolfe argues that, whereas wealthy individuals used to give large bequests to build churches and fund religious programs, that money is now often given to support the arts.[19]

The difficulty that the Christian artist faces is that the expectations of the Christian community and those of the artistic community will almost inevitably clash. At Wheaton, one form this clash takes is the continuing question: "Why can't students paint nude models?" Yet there are many other points of tension, ones that I don't see as going away anytime soon. Artists are often viewed as "different" and thus not easily integrable into the more generic Christian community. To some extent, this is true, normal, and to be expected. Consider what Irving Stone says about artists:

> But then, no artist is normal: if he were, he wouldn't be an artist.
> Normal men don't create works of art. They eat, sleep, hold down
> routine jobs, and die. You [the artist] are hypersensitive to life and
> nature; that's why you are able to interpret for the rest of us. But
> if you are not careful, that very hypersensitiveness will lead you to
> your destruction. The strain of it breaks every artist in time.[20]

Of course, as we have already seen, there is a real danger of overstating the difference of artists from "regular" folks. This quotation comes from a rather famous book that has done much to popularize the life of Van Gogh, but it also has helped promote the idea of the "struggling artist," who finds it hard to have a place in the community. Yet we have seen that Van Gogh should hardly be taken as paradigmatic for all artists everywhere. There is no doubt that Van Gogh was hypersensitive and that his hypersensitiveness was part of his destruction. But it is unwise to generalize regarding all artists on the basis of Van Gogh's experience. Indeed, I have argued that, in a very important sense, we are *all* artists. To be sure, some of us are called very specifically to an artistic vocation or avocation. Those artists who are so called do sometimes promote such an overstatement since, in some respects, it makes them feel "different" (and, given the way the term "different" is often used, "superior"). There is no question that artists often *do* have a kind

19. Tom Wolfe, "The Worship of Art: Notes on a New God," *Harper's* 289 (October 1984): 61–68.

20. Irving Stone, *Lust for Life* (Garden City, NY: Doubleday, 1934), 350.

of sensitivity that many others lack, though we need to be careful of exactly what we make of this. Truly, we should celebrate the kinds of sensitivities that artists have, but we should not forget that others have other valuable sensitivities that are equally beneficial to their communities.

In any case, these sensitivities often create a degree of tension between the artist and her religious community. What one does about that tension is, I think, the crucial question. One of Asher's failings—in my opinion—is that he never really faces up to this tension. He seems caught in the middle—like a deer in the headlights—and reacts more than acts, or simply doesn't act at all. Did he have to paint that crucifixion scene of his mother? Perhaps he did. Did he have to show the picture publicly? Perhaps so. Yet it's not completely clear in what sense he "had" to do so. What is never articulated clearly in the book is exactly *why* there is this necessity for his expression of truth, as he feels it, to take that form.

In any case, if one wishes to avoid playing the whore, one must be intentional about how one negotiates the tensions between communities. Part of that negotiation is that one must inevitably partake of that dirty little word: "compromise." If being an artist is living between these worlds—and if those respective worlds demand a certain allegiance of their members—then one must decide in what ways that allegiance will be attenuated. If one is a Christian, then one should have questions about accepting the goal implied by Robert Henri when he says, "Every great artist is a man who has freed himself from his family, his nation, his race." First, it's not at all clear that all great artists have done this. One might, instead, argue that many or even *most* great artists were great precisely because they found their place in the community. Bach immediately comes to mind. Second, even if some artists have found greatness in thrusting aside their connection to their communities, that hardly means that *all* artists will only find greatness by so doing. Third, should "greatness" (whatever that may be) truly require this disconnection, then perhaps Christians simply don't have that option available to them. It is hard to see a justification for art that doesn't include at least *some* sense of being responsible to the Christian community, even if that sense of responsibility can be worked out in various ways.

So far I've been talking as if there are such clear entities as "the artist" and "the audience" or "the community." But, of course, things are never as neat and uncomplicated as that. We are all part of multiple and diverse communities, some of which are within the general confines of what we call "the church." As a Christian artist, I can (and indeed to some extent *must*) choose which community I will direct my art to. For it is very difficult—if not impossible—to create art that is for all communities (my extended family, the next-door neighbors, people I know from my workplace, people with whom I attend church, folks from my Bible study group, etc.). One possibility is to direct my art simply to the art world, and that's a choice that some Christian artists take. But it's important to see that this doesn't really mean that one is now "free." Instead, one has chosen to work within the confines—that is, the limitations and expectations—of the art world. Often artists see themselves as "free" because they've adopted the standards of the art world. But, as it turns out, the art world is oppressive in its own way. One need only think of the stereotypical ways that artists are expected to "be"—let alone what they can and cannot paint, sculpt, or compose—to make that clear. Another possibility is that I direct my art at a particular segment of the Christian community. That, too, involves working within certain confines. In either case, I can say "my art is not directed toward *them*" (whoever "them" might be) and is instead directed toward this group (or these other groups).

Yet there is another side to this whole equation. We have been speaking here largely of the artist's responsibility to a community (or multiple communities). But clearly that responsibility goes both ways—in other words, *communities* have responsibilities to *artists*. One way to work this out is in terms of church communities responding to artists in their midst. In the previous chapter, I mentioned a number of churches that have made a point of incorporating art and artists into the life of the church. Of course, one of the important things to keep in mind here is that not all art is equally accessible. True, historically art has been made in such a way that it was immediately evident to viewers and listeners. The makers of stained-glass windows in medieval churches were hardly interested in depicting something so sophisticated that viewers would need an education just to make sense of it. Indeed, historically most communities would have had the tools to make sense of art, if for no other reason than because they (both artists and communities) were so enmeshed in the same cultural practices that easy communication would have been presupposed. Yet artists today often make art that is *not* designed to be immediately accessible. Instead, such art often requires some degree of education to make sense of it. Yet, oddly enough, when people visit their local art museum or concert hall, they expect that all art should be immediately accessible to them. However, if one thinks of this requirement more closely, it seems rather strange: no one would think that a philosopher or theologian or physicist should only write texts that are immediately accessible to the general public. In fact, we tend to assume the opposite: we simply don't expect experts writing on, say, nuclear science to be accessible to the average person. To be sure, there may well be artists who simply do not care if the general public can understand their art. Perhaps there is something elitist in that, but I'm not sure. Milton Babbitt (1916–2011) wrote a rather famous article titled "Who Cares If You Listen?" in which he explained that he was writing his rather complicated music for only his ten or fifteen friends who could understand it.[21] Not surprisingly, that article generated a huge controversy, not least because readers thought that Babbitt was all too exemplary of a shameful disregard for listeners and viewers. In fact, the article was taken to be indicative of the general sense of artists and their regard for the public. Yet Babbitt—however elitist he might seem—is simply making a kind of choice: he has chosen to write his music for his very close circle of friends. In the same way, all artists need to make choices as to which audience(s) they are attempting to reach, and then they need to be attentive as to how best to reach them. But that doesn't let the listener or viewer off the hook: we are likewise responsible to be thoughtful listeners or viewers—ones who take the necessary time and expend the energy to engage with art that has been set before us. Obviously, there needs to be a kind of ongoing negotiation here.

Ultimately, as a Christian, my responsibility as an artist is toward God. That may mean that I create art simply in praise of God, perhaps art that no one else will ever see, like gargoyles on tops of cathedrals. Such art is just as valid as that made for the community. But, having said that, I should add that I am uncomfortable with the notion of being true to "one's art," which Henri emphasizes so

21. Milton Babbitt, "Who Cares If You Listen?" *High Fidelity*, February 1958, 38–40. It should be pointed out that Babbitt had originally titled the article "The Composer as Specialist," which was changed by an editor without Babbitt's permission. See Anthony Tommasini, "Finding Still More Life in a 'Dead' Idiom," *New York Times*, October 6, 1996, H39.

strongly. Perhaps there is some way of making sense of this ideal, but it seems to me that one can only meaningfully be true to one-self, to another person, or to God. As far as I can see, being true to one's art—which is in effect an ethical obligation—can only be made sense of if it is construed in terms of being true to *someone*.

Making the World "Pretty"

Responsibility to a community need not take any simple form along the lines of "as an artist, I should simply give the audience what it wants." Being responsive to the needs of an audience ("responsive" as in "responsibility") doesn't necessarily mean that one gives it exactly what it wants. On the other hand, it likewise doesn't mean that we have the goal of giving the audience precisely what it *doesn't* want. The difficulty comes in finding the compromise with which one can live responsibly. As Christians, perhaps some of us would like for artists to "make the world pretty." There is probably a place for that sort of art, in the same way that there is a place for what R. G. Collingwood called "amusement art" or any art that allows for "escape." Escapism as a way of life may be bad, but escapism as one of its moments shouldn't trouble us. Highbrow folks sometimes speak condescendingly of the masses who seek out films that are "escapist." Disneyland is often mentioned in the same breath. But even highbrow folks have their own respective highbrow "escapes."

Yet artists may well need to respond to an audience's needs by giving them what they do *not* want. If the world isn't pretty, then pretty pictures—at least in one important sense—aren't really *true*. They may depict a reality of the *eschaton* but not reality as we know it here. Perhaps the greatest temptation of the Christian artist is to *lie*—to make life prettier than it really is. That temptation raises the age-old problem already presented by Plato, whose primary complaint about artists is that they lie. The distinction that Plato makes is that, whereas philosophers give us "the truth" as it is, artists merely tell us stories about the world that come in varying degrees of verisimilitude. Oddly enough, though, Plato *himself* justifies lying as long as it serves the purposes of bettering the youth, for he claims that it is better to tell children stories in which the good guys always win (even while realizing that, in truth, the good guys *don't* always win). That kind of justification is all too

common among Christians, though it is one that artists should
resist. We like stories with happy endings, but ones with sad endings are often—sadly—more true to life. Responsibility need not
mean that we never disturb anyone else, but it does mean that we
do not do so without good reason. And deciding what counts as
"good reason" is sometimes difficult.

All of this returns us to the question of "beauty." Any reader who
knows much about the world of fine art realizes that beauty has been
a kind of taboo for quite some time. The title of Wendy Steiner's
book *Venus in Exile: The Rejection of Beauty in 20th Century Art*
describes the situation well.[22] But what was so bad about beauty?
One problem was that "beautiful" had been all too connected to
"pretty" or "sweet" in most artists' and critics' minds. If a piece of
art were declared "beautiful," that would have been the equivalent
of saying that it was "superficial" or "sentimental." In short, the
problem was that such art was deemed escapist and, in an important sense, "untrue." For, if art is to be "realistic" and the world
as we experience it is flawed and fallen, then art should reflect this.

Not surprisingly, then, "good" art for about the past century or
so has often been expected to be shocking and subversive. Anything
less than this has been taken to be less than "true" and "realistic."
One of the most memorable quotes regarding the purpose of modern art is that of Barnett Newman, who writes, "The impulse of
modern art is to destroy beauty."[23] Of course, the easiest ways to
destroy beauty are to depict ugliness and to shock. We have already
seen that some modern art is provocative—at least seemingly—just
to be provocative. Indeed, art has become increasingly shocking.
Another problem, though, has been that of aesthetic relativism (i.e.,
relativism with respect to the truth of the *beauty* of art), which
we noted (in chapter 2) goes back to Kant. As long as "beauty"
is merely a sentiment that we feel and not something true of the
object we experience, then it would seem that aesthetic relativism
is almost inevitable.

Yet, as far back as 1996, Peter Schjeldahl declared that "beauty is
back."[24] One of the more important manifestations of that return

22. Wendy Schneider, *Venus in Exile: The Rejection of Beauty in 20th Century Art*
(New York: Free Press, 2001).

23. Barnett Newman, "The Sublime Is Now," *Tiger's Eye* 1 (1948): 52.

24. Peter Schjeldahl, "Beauty Is Back: A Trampled Esthetic Blooms Again," *New
York Times Magazine*, September 29, 1996, 161.

was the appearance of Elaine Scarry's book *On Beauty and Being Just*. There she argues that what she took to be the two major arguments against beauty were simply false. The first argument is that beauty "distracts attention from wrong social arrangements."[25] In other words, we become so preoccupied with the beautiful that we forget about the realities of the human condition. The remedy for this, of course, is that art become "realistic," depicting life in its nitty-gritty truth. Admittedly, there *is* always a danger of being distracted by the beautiful, yet beauty in no way *necessitates* that distraction. The second argument Scarry mentions is that staring at a beautiful object somehow degrades it. This argument is even more problematic than the first. Perhaps this would be true if the object depicted is an actual person, but it is hard to think of most other things that are depicted in art (landscapes, animals, or flowers) as being degraded by such depiction. Indeed, one could argue that staring at such depictions generally celebrates and *enhances* precisely what is being depicted. In any case, shows such as *Regarding Beauty: A View of the Late 20th Century* at the Hirshhorn Museum and Sculpture Gallery in Washington, DC, around the turn of the century, mark this remarkable change in how beauty is perceived.

And that leads us to aesthetic relativism. As far as I can tell, it is flourishing as much as ever. Earlier, I mentioned how often I find this idea among my students. For them, of course, the Bible clearly mandates *ethical* absolutism but says nothing about relativism of an aesthetic sort. And yet, I remind them of God calling Bezalel and Oholiab to be artists. Regarding Bezalel, God says, "I have filled him with divine spirit, with ability, intelligence, and knowledge in every kind of craft" (Exod. 31:3). This hardly sounds like a statement made by an aesthetic relativist. Moreover, when one considers God's exacting standards for the tabernacle that Bezalel and Oholiab were instructed to build, it becomes quite clear that God has rather high standards for what he considers beautiful.

Of course, there are other reasons why aesthetic relativism, even while perhaps *appearing* to be a valid position, simply isn't an attractive option. If one is really an aesthetic relativist, then *any* piece of art—no matter how poorly executed—is ultimately just as good as any other. In fact, if you were a true aesthetic relativist, then

25. Elaine Scarry, *On Beauty and Being Just* (Princeton, NJ: Princeton University Press, 1999), 58.

you would have to maintain that there is no superiority gained by *practicing*, for a beginning piano student is just as good as a concert pianist. Yet no thinking person would endorse that. A major stumbling block for many on this issue is the confusion of "liking" with "being good." Often what people really mean when they endorse aesthetic relativism is that there are no *likings* that are better than any others. To a great extent, that's true (though, obviously, a liking for art that degrades or is blatantly untrue is problematic). One person may prefer classical music, another country. But preference or liking is not the same as saying that something is good. In fact, I might well acknowledge that Picasso is one of the greatest painters of all time without saying I like Picasso and want to have one of his paintings hanging in my living room. There are all kinds of art that I personally acknowledge as excellent but that I don't really want to view or listen to on a regular basis. Yet that preference is not the same as the acknowledgment of aesthetic quality. I greatly enjoy reading novels by P. G. Wodehouse—he's a master of English style and he's really funny. But I hardly think that Wodehouse is *therefore* one of the great writers of all time. Additionally, the assumption is often made that there is something like "the standards" by which all music or painting or theater must be judged. Yet, on even a rather brief deliberation, this proves false, for what makes a piece of classical music excellent is not necessarily what makes a piece of reggae excellent. Actually, even the idea that pieces of jazz or given improvisations can be meaningfully compared must be qualified, for two different jazz improvisations may have quite different qualities about them that make them *both* excellent. Finally, in judging a piece of art, we often need to ask, "What does the maker of this piece of art intend it to do?" We noted in chapter 2 that the modern discourse of art chopped off "use" as a way of judging art. Yet it is surely one aspect by which we may and even should judge art. For example, there is a long tradition in classical music of *Tafelmusik* (literally "table music" but really "music to eat by"). To judge *Tafelmusik* by standards such as "complexity" or "attention grabbing" would be simply to misunderstand the genre. The music is *supposed* to be background music. One is not supposed to listen to it closely. Instead, it is designed to heighten the pleasure of eating and conversing. Or, to put this another way, I have on occasion been invited to people's houses for dinner at which they played music that was most decidedly *not* designed to

be background music—a Beethoven symphony or, even worse, a
Wagnerian opera. Whether or not you like Richard Wagner, his
music simply doesn't encourage the kind of atmosphere condu-
cive for dining and conversation. So, on my view, there *is* a kind of
relativism, but it is relativism that has everything to do with what
genre a piece of art is and what it is intended to be. For instance,
Dylan's way of singing is great for protest songs, which is why you
wouldn't really want to hear Luciano Pavarotti doing a Dylan cover
(a thought that's all too troubling).[26]

So there *are* standards for beauty, even if they are more complicated and more genre-related than often recognized. Once we
acknowledge that beauty truly exists and that there are standards
for beauty, our attitude toward it changes remarkably. Scarry notes
that "beauty quickens. It adrenalizes. It makes the heart beat faster.
It makes life more vivid, animated, living, worth living."[27] I heart-
ily agree.

Yet, having said that there really *is* beauty and that there *are*
standards by which it may be judged, we are still left with the fact
that our world is not one of unequivocal beauty. For what is the
status of beauty in the midst of a fallen world, in which all is not
necessarily beautiful, good, or true? And what is the artist to *do* in
such a world? It's easy to think that one has made the world more
holy by creating yet another Christian trinket. Yet the artist is certainly faced with a difficult situation. The world is still—in many
ways—as God pronounced it: "good." And yet, it is so full of that
which is "not good." Traditionally, artists have particularly focused
on that which is beautiful in the world, whether the human figure or
the natural landscape or pleasing harmonies. It has been only more
recently (and "recent" here is defined in terms of the long history
of Western art) that artists have turned their attention to subjects
that are not traditionally thought to be "beautiful." While there is
no question that some art that is created today is shocking just to
be shocking and vile just to be vile, it is likewise the case that artists who, say, paint that which is not beautiful in some traditional
sense do so out of a deep commitment to truth.

26. Some of the "best" material from Jim Nayder's "Annoying Music Show" is
exactly this sort of thing (Johnny Cash singing "I Walk the Line" in German or William Shatner "singing" "It Was a Very Good Year").
27. Scarry, *On Beauty and Being Just*, 24.

In speaking of Johannes Brahms's (1833–97) *Requiem* and John Coltrane's (1926–67) *A Love Supreme*, Cornel West observes:

> Music at its best achieves this summit because it is the grand arche-ology into and transfiguration of our guttural cry, the great human effort to grasp in time . . . our deepest passions and yearnings as prisoners of time. Profound music leads us—beyond language—to the dark roots of our scream and the celestial heights of our silence.[28]

West terms his own viewpoint "Chekhovian Christian," in that he sees himself as a Christian who has taken seriously the tragic condi-tions that we find ourselves in as depicted by the playwright Anton Chekhov (1860–1904), whose plays very clearly emphasize the tragic nature of human existence. West insists that, from a Christian point of view, "despair and hope are inseparable. One can never under-stand what hope is really about unless one wrestles with despair. The same is true with faith. There has to be some serious doubt, otherwise faith becomes merely a dogmatic formula, an orthodoxy, a way of evading the complexity of life, rather than a way of engag-ing honestly with life."[29] It is this engaging with both sides—hope and despair, faith and doubt, beauty and brokenness—that keeps us honest. To focus on one to the exclusion of the other is to miss the fullness of human existence.

Art that takes beauty seriously is art that takes tragedy seriously. Dmitry Shostakovich's (1906–75) symphonies are not necessar-ily "pretty," but they are faithful witnesses (the thirteenth, for example) to the horrors of his time in the Soviet Union. Here we might be tempted to say that such music puts greater emphasis on the true than on the beautiful. But it is not that the beauti-ful has simply been neglected; rather, we witness a sense of the beautiful that is not simply that of Kant's harmonious free play of the faculties. Ultimately, we can agree with Daniel A. Siedell, when he writes:

> Artistic practice, then, is utopian. It recognizes that the world is not as it should be. And it therefore projects alternative worlds. Russian filmmaker Andrei Tarkovsky once said, echoing Dostoyevsky and other Russian thinkers, that if the world were perfect there would

28. Cornel West, *The Cornel West Reader* (New York: Basic, 2000), xvii.
29. Ibid., 554.

be no need for art. Art is a witness to both our fallen world and hope for its redemption.[30]

What unites Christian artists like those whose work was part of the exhibition "A Broken Beauty" is that they depict *both* "suffering and hope," *both* "human brokenness and human beauty."[31] And here we can make a strong connection to both African American spirituals and improvisers. So many of the spirituals speak of both suffering and hope with a recognition that we are currently captives but that freedom looms on the horizon. So we have "Swing Low, Sweet Chariot" that is "comin' for to carry me home." Or "Steal Away," which ends with the line: "I ain't got long to stay here." There is clearly an eschatological hope in these spirituals, both for the more immediate *eschaton* of escape from slavery and for the ultimate *eschaton* of being "home." Likewise, African American jazz improvisers have seen their music as a way to "overwrite, resist, and confound both conventional musical practices and the orthodox social structures those practices reflect."[32] Many African American improvisers have seen their work as undermining repressive, white social structures. And, indeed, it was partly due to the respect that improvisers slowly gained that African Americans in general gained dignity in American culture. Houston A. Baker says of the blues that they transformed the "economics of slavery" into a "resonant, improvisational, expressive dignity."[33] We could likewise say that jazz has helped transform the "economics of oppression" into a similar sort of dignity.

Ultimately, we refuse to "sell out" when we are willing to be people of integrity and tell the truth. As we have seen, this is much more difficult than it might at first seem. To tell the truth means to present the world as it is, refusing to lie. It is to avoid anything

---

30. Daniel A. Siedell, *God in the Gallery: A Christian Embrace of Modern Art* (Grand Rapids: Baker Academic, 2008), 29.

31. Timothy Verdon, "Broken Beauty, Shattered Heart," in *A Broken Beauty*, ed. Theodore L. Prescott (Grand Rapids: Eerdmans, 2005), 25. The exhibit has been at the Laguna Art Museum in Laguna Beach and the Joseph D. Carrier Gallery in Toronto.

32. Daniel Fischlin and Ajay Heble, "The Other Side of Nowhere: Jazz, Improvisation, and Communities in Dialogue," in *The Other Side of Nowhere: Jazz, Improvisation, and Communities in Dialogue*, ed. Daniel Fischlin and Ajay Heble (Middletown, CT: Wesleyan University Press, 2004), 2.

33. Houston A. Baker Jr., *Blues, Ideology, and Afro-American Literature: A Vernacular Theory* (Chicago: University of Chicago Press, 1984), 13.

easy and cliché. It is to speak both of brokenness and of hope. We point to that which is true now and that which will be true one day. This is why we can call the artistic vocation *prophetic*: prophets speak the truth to their communities. But how do they speak that truth? The answer is: our lives and our art become *icons* that point to God. What it means for our lives to be icons is the question to which we now turn.

Becoming Living
Works of Art[1]

"The practice of the liturgy means that by the help of grace, under the guidance of the Church, we grow into living works of art before God, with no other aim or purpose than that of living and existing in His sight."[2] Whether we agree with Romano Guardini that our existence is *only* for God's sake—although it clearly is for God's sake first and foremost—his insight into the nature of liturgy is profound and true. As we have seen, liturgy properly defined is all about our becoming living works of art. Much of that takes place in "everyday life," though it is also deeply intertwined with what we do when we gather more formally as a Christian community—for the growth that takes place in liturgy is profoundly communal. Indeed, as Alexander Schmemann notes, the very meaning of *leitourgia* is "an action by which a group of people become something corporately which they had not been as a mere collection of individuals—a whole greater than the sum of its parts."[3]

1. I gratefully dedicate this chapter to Bob Webber, a great influence on my life and my thoughts about worship.
2. Romano Guardini, *The Spirit of the Liturgy*, trans. Ada Lane (New York: Continuum, 1998), 71.
3. Alexander Schmemann, *For the Life of the World*, 2nd ed. (Crestwood, NY: St. Vladimir's Seminary Press, 1973), 25.

In the introduction, we noted the distinction between "intensive liturgy" and "extensive liturgy." On the one hand, intensive liturgy is "what happens when Christians assemble to worship God." Within intensive liturgy, we meet the living Christ by way of Word and sacrament. Through intensive liturgy, we are taught, sustained, and fed. On the other hand, extensive liturgy is "what happens when Christians leave the assembly to conduct their daily affairs." We are sustained and fed precisely in order to go out into the world. Of course, these two kinds of liturgy are wholly dependent upon one another. It is not as if we could have one without the other. "As our intensive liturgies drive us into the world to do our extensive liturgies, so our extensive liturgies bring us back week by week to the Christian assembly."[4] There is a kind of play between intensive and extensive liturgy, with each leading us back to the other.

Extensive Liturgy

I opened the introduction with the following claim: "I think it is safe to say that there is nothing more basic to human existence than the call and response structure. It is, quite simply, the very structure of our lives." I trust at this point that this claim would seem so true as to be simply obvious. We are called into being and our lives constitute our response. Moreover, our lives are filled with calls—from God, from fellow believers, from our parents and family, from friends, from teachers and professors. There is no aspect of our lives from which the call and response pattern is absent.

As part of this call into being, we are called to present our lives and bodies as living works of art. Although Saint Paul speaks explicitly of "your bodies as a living sacrifice" (Rom. 12:1), surely our minds must be included. After all, Jesus tells us that the greatest commandment is: "You shall love the Lord your God with all your heart, and with all your soul, and with all your mind" (Matt. 22:37). In short, Jesus calls us to love God with all of our being. We have seen that, as beings created in God's image, we are called to be creative improvisers in all that we do. For we are God's *poiēma*—the work of his hands—and we are given not merely the gift of life but also the gift of being able to mold that life. To expand on what it

4. Charles P. Price and Louis Weil, *Liturgy for Living* (New York: Seabury, 1979), 297.

means to shape and mold our lives, we have considered the notion of improvisation. I have argued that, although we are not properly creators in the way that God is, we *are* improvisers who constantly improvise upon ourselves and upon the world. Indeed, living life is precisely this improvisation, even if we do not realize or appreciate it. Our call, then, is to take this gift of improvisation seriously as we shape our lives—not simply by ourselves but in community—into lives that glorify God.

I have put these notions of call and improvisation into the overarching category of "liturgy," since liturgy is central to our lives. Here I want to develop that notion more clearly in terms of extensive liturgy; in the second half of the chapter, I will turn to intensive liturgy.

In chapter 1, we saw that Chrysostom thinks of our growing in grace as analogous to the way that paintings or pieces of sculpture develop. In such a way, we become living works of art, as Guardini puts it. Parents are commended to think of rearing their children in terms of making artworks. Accordingly, children are called to continue that improvisatory work upon themselves, in conjunction with others in the Christian community. Chrysostom also encourages catechumens—those preparing for baptism and entry into the church—to consider their souls to be paintings.

> As therefore happens in the case of painters from life, so let it happen in your case. For they, arranging their boards, and tracing white lines upon them, and sketching the royal likeness in outline, before they apply the actual colors, rub out some lines, and change some for others, rectifying mistakes, and altering what is amiss with all freedom. But when they put on the coloring for good, it is no longer in their power to rub out again, and to change one thing for another, since they injure the beauty of the portrait, and the result becomes an eyesore. Consider that your soul is the portrait; before therefore the true coloring of the spirit comes, wipe out habits which have wrongly been implanted. . . . Correct your habits, so that when the colors are applied, and the royal likeness is brought out, you may no more wipe them out in the future; and add damage and scars to the beauty which has been given you by God.[5]

5. John Chrysostom, *Instructions to Catechumens*, trans. W. R. W. Stephens and T. P. Brandram, in *Nicene and Post-Nicene Fathers*, series 1, vol. 9, ed. Philip Schaff (Buffalo, NY: Christian Literature, 1889), 2.3.

Baptism here is likened to adding coloring to a piece of canvas: before the color can be applied, the sketch lines must be straight and true. So also with our lives: they must be properly shaped and molded. Yet Chrysostom is hardly alone in this way of thinking. In a very similar fashion, Basil of Ancyra speaks not only of the virgin's soul as like a canvas but also of all that is external—how she acts and her body—as being a work of art.[6] The goal here is to be more and more conformed, so that she becomes an image of God. Put only slightly differently, her goal is to become an *icon*, pointing to God rather than to herself. And these are just a few examples of a way of thinking about our souls and bodies in terms of art that has been common throughout the Christian tradition.

Of course, Chrysostom and Basil are writing in a way that is very much conditioned by their times. The idea that one saw one's own person as an artwork was common, whether one was a pagan, a Jew, or a Christian. The question "What would Jesus do?" is fairly new,[7] but its form is quite old. The ancient Stoic philosopher Epictetus writes (in the second century AD), "When you are about to meet someone, especially someone who seems to be distinguished, put to yourself the question, 'What would Socrates or Zeno have done in these circumstances?'"[8] The point of studying ancient texts was to become different persons. As Peter Brown observes about readers in late antiquity, "The Classics, a literary tradition, existed for the sole purpose of 'making [persons] into classics': exposure to the classics of Greek and Latin literature was intended to produce exemplary beings, their raw humanity molded and filed away by a double discipline, at once ethical and aesthetic."[9] The goal was to find exemplary authors and figures to emulate—and then to do so. So the idea of seeing oneself as a piece of art or a "classic" is a very old idea.

Yet what does this mean in terms of living artistically? Here I want to connect *leitourgia* with two other ancient Greek terms that are similar in important ways. One term is *mousikē*, which we translate as "music." But, whereas "music" refers to a quite specific discipline,

6. Basil of Ancyra, *De virg.* 36 (PG 30:740D–741A). See Teresa M. Shaw, "Askesis and the Appearance of Holiness," *Journal of Early Christian Studies* 6 (1998): 492–93.
7. Charles Sheldon, *In His Steps: What Would Jesus Do?* (first published in serial form by the *Chicago Advance* in 1897).
8. Epictetus, *Handbook*, trans. Nicholas P. White (Indianapolis: Hackett, 1983), 23.
9. Peter Brown, "The Saint as Exemplar in Late Antiquity," *Representations* 1 (1983): 1.

mousikē refers to the broader discipline of cultivating oneself as a whole. Although "practicing music" can mean to compose or perform music, it has the much broader meaning of cultivating the soul. It is through the concept of *mousikē* that the narrow sense of being an artist (creating paintings, pieces of sculpture, or works of music) and the broad sense (becoming a work of art oneself) are brought together. For, given the Socratic conception of *mousikē*, life is ultimately about the cultivation of the soul. Both the ancient Greeks and the early Christians realized that one cultivates the self by way of spiritual disciplines or exercises. The philosopher Pierre Hadot reminds us that, for ancient philosophers, "philosophy" meant "living a certain kind of way." Hadot argues that philosophy was equivalent to practicing the spiritual disciplines, or *askēsis* (the ancient Greek term for spiritual exercise), which are designed so that we "*let* ourselves be changed, in our point of view, attitudes, and convictions. This means that we must dialogue with ourselves, and hence do battle with ourselves." Clearly, *askēsis* is a thoroughgoing process that involves our very being in the deepest possible sense. Hadot describes the result of *askēsis* as "a conversion which turns our entire life upside down, changing the life of the person who goes through it."[10] The Christian word for "conversion" is *metanoia*, which literally means a change of mind but indicates a complete change of life. It carries with it the idea of a 180-degree turn—an utter reversal of the direction of one's life. While Christians tend to think that "spiritual disciplines" are something unique to Christianity, the reality is that such disciplines predated the advent of Christianity. Thus, Christians imported such disciplines from pagan philosophy and Judaism, adapting them for distinctively Christian ends.

It is important to make clear at the outset that the "spiritual" in spiritual disciplines does *not* mean that such exercises are either mental or pertaining to the soul; instead, they involve the whole person—body and soul. Philo of Alexandria provides us with two lists of exercises. Consider the following: research, investigation, reading, listening, attention, self-mastery, and indifference to indifferent things.[11] Probably the most important of these categories is that

10. Pierre Hadot, *Philosophy as a Way of Life: Spiritual Exercises from Socrates to Foucault*, ed. Arnold I. Davidson, trans. Michael Chase (Oxford: Blackwell, 1995), 91, 83.
11. Ibid., 84.

of "attention," or self-awareness. What the Stoics called *prosokhē* (attention) "supposes that, at each instant, we renew our choice of life . . . and that we keep constantly present in our minds the rules of life which express that choice."[12] Given that Paul exhorts us not to be "conformed to this world" but instead to "be transformed" (Rom. 12:2), such attention is surely appropriate. We must constantly be aware of ourselves, of our motives and actions. Under the category of listening, we could place both prayer and meditation. When we engage in meditation, we allow God to speak to us, and we ruminate upon Christian teachings about how we ought to live. For the Stoics, meditation involves remembering and even memorizing key maxims, dwelling upon them, and seeing how they can be put into practice. The point of meditation is to transform both our thinking and our practice. Meditating on the fruit of the Spirit (for example) can provide us with insight as to how we can *live out* such characteristics as patience and self-control. Indeed, Saint Paul calls us to think on those things that will lift up our gaze and our lives: "Whatever is true, whatever is honorable, whatever is just, whatever is pure, whatever is pleasing, whatever is commendable, if there is any excellence and if there is anything worthy of praise, think about these things" (Phil. 4:8). Then he goes on to connect these meditations to practice: "Keep on doing the things that you have learned and received and heard and seen in me, and the God of peace will be with you" (Phil. 4:9). Research, investigation, and reading all involve immersing ourselves in the truths of the Christian faith and considering how these truths should be expressed practically. Reading Scripture is clearly central to a distinctively Christian *askēsis*, but so is reading theology or classic Christian texts. We are also involved in research and investigation when we speak with fellow believers about living the life of faith or when we seek out the counsel of someone who is truly wise and mature in the faith.

I find it highly revealing that the pianist John Bayless devotes much of his day to distinctly Christian *askēsis*: spending time in prayer, reading the Bible and devotional literature, and keeping a journal. As he puts it: "I only spend an hour (at most) per day playing the piano."[13] Here it couldn't be more clear that becoming a certain

12. Pierre Hadot, *What Is Ancient Philosophy?* trans. Michael Chase (Cambridge, MA: Harvard, 2002), 193.
13. This quote is taken from a personal interview with John Bayless in June 2007.

kind of person is key to his musicianship. Doing distinctly "artistic" things is certainly important, but it is even more fundamental to work on the artistry of becoming a "living sacrifice." Our first and foremost project is working with God to become his works of art. As should be clear, there is a kind of circular character to such ways of being. We become patient by actually attempting to live out patience. Our efforts at first are often halting, but there is no other way to become patient than to learn patience in little things and to work our way up from there. It is only in this back-and-forth movement that we develop what the Stoics call "self-mastery." Of course, here it is important to add that the Christian conception of self-mastery has a twist: we become truly who we ought to be by *relinquishing* our insistence on mastering ourselves and allowing ourselves to be mastered by *God*. In this sense, we become artists alongside of God. For those who are artists in the more narrow sense of that term, there is the potential for a wonderful merging of the artistic work that we do on our souls and bodies and that which is done on canvas or with words. For that artistic work can *itself* become a way of praying and praising. Like Bezalel, who was called to be an artist and was filled with the Spirit, artists can work out their calling through the prayer of artistic activity. Being artistic becomes not merely a fundamental way of being in the world but also a special calling for certain people. For those who are so called, writing poetry or painting canvases becomes its own kind of *askēsis*.

While there are differences between the terms *mousikē*, *askēsis*, and *leitourgia*, they all involve living in such a way that we are changed.[14] Of course, *leitourgia* adds the crucial dimension of living our lives in service both to God and to our neighbors. Moreover, it puts particular emphasis on the communal nature of this work: we minister to members of the body of Christ as a community. Here we have the intermingling of the senses of the extensive and intensive meanings of "liturgy"—those of daily living and corporate worship. As should become clear, the two are not in any way mutually exclusive. Instead, they feed upon one another. If we are living as godly works of art, then corporate worship and the worship that we render to God by living our lives will mingle with each other so that it becomes impossible to separate them. It is highly

---

14. I discuss *mousikē* and *askēsis* at length in Bruce Ellis Benson, "Nietzsche's Musical *Askesis* for Resisting Decadence," *Journal of Nietzsche Studies* 34 (2007): 28–46.

appropriate, then, that Rory Noland speaks of "the church as a colony of artists."[15] But let me expand what he says even further: for, if we are all artists together, then that colony is constituted by the way we live as a *collective*. We are all striving together to become works of art that are pleasing to God and examples to the world.

Yet, not only are the two senses of *liturgy* connected; liturgy of both types is strongly connected to the arts. Artists in the more narrow sense of the term are certainly among those who help us think about God in new and helpful ways. In attempting to visualize God, the saints, or the Christian life, the arts can challenge our current ways of thinking about God. Earlier, we considered Marion's distinction between the icon and the idol. When I mentioned that distinction to Buddy Owens, pastor of spiritual growth at Saddleback Church, he immediately responded, "A worship leader is an icon."[16] I think that nicely sums it up. Whatever is part of a worship service—whether a sermon or art—needs to be iconic, pointing beyond itself. Even though it has value in and of itself (I in no way mean to suggest a simplistic utilitarianism), in the context of worship, that artistic value is not the focus, however significant it may be. Or perhaps we should put that slightly differently: the artistic value of a piece of art *within the context of worship* becomes precisely its value as an aid to worship. The extent to which it aids worship—not drawing attention to itself but instead directing us to the holy—is its primary artistic value in that context. As we will see, intensive liturgy is infused with artistic elements at every turn.

Before we turn to the various elements of intensive liturgy, we need to consider its basic structure. Robert E. Webber memorably describes worship by saying that it "does God's story."[17] In other words, intensive worship is intensely *performative* in nature. Liturgical actions are not just add-ons. Instead, we "perform" the Gospel story each time we enact it. When we celebrate God's story, we proclaim it afresh. We remember the past and anticipate the future. We eat the bread and drink the cup because Jesus has invited us to do so. And we do all of this in a way that is heavily dependent upon the senses—not just the mind—and thus the arts. It is not too much

15. Rory Noland, *The Heart of the Artist* (Grand Rapids: Zondervan, 1999), 89.
16. From a conversation with Buddy Owens in June 2007.
17. Robert E. Webber, *Ancient-Future Worship: Proclaiming and Enacting God's Narrative* (Grand Rapids: Baker, 2008), 20.

to say that our worship is infused with the arts at every point. For our worship is not just for our souls but also for our bodies. It is designed to engage us both mentally and by way of our senses, with each reinforcing the other. Richard D. McCall explains this movement in terms of *enactment*: "The enacted or liturgical manner . . . takes embodied action in time and space to be the only adequate locus for confronting the reality of human life in time and space and thus the only adequate locus in which to meet the God whose Word is made flesh to dwell among us."[18] Given that we worship an incarnate God, we should expect nothing less. The words that we say and the actions that we do are deeply connected. Thus, we can say that "sacramental words and gestures are not simply the embodiment of some thought. Like tangible things, they are themselves the carriers of their meaning, which is inseparable from its material form."[19]

We shall better understand this basic form as we consider intensive liturgy in detail.

Intensive Liturgy

As one approaches Saint Gregory of Nyssa Episcopal Church in San Francisco, it is virtually impossible not to be stopped—and warmly greeted—by someone on the front steps. Even before one enters the physical building we call the "church," the *ekklēsia* (the Greek word for "church," which means the people rather than a building) literally surrounds one. That is entirely appropriate, for the mere physical building is only a gathering place for the *ekklēsia*. Saint Gregory's is a remarkable place aesthetically: it is clearly designed to affect all of the senses. One enters a large octagonal space and discovers a dramatic icon of dancing saints. The Cappadocian Father Saint Gregory of Nyssa—the namesake of the church—commended dancing as an important part of worship. Of course, there are icons throughout the church, along with festive Ethiopian crosses and lamps from India. Saint Gregory's is an excellent example of how art and its appeal to the senses have been used to enhance the

18. Richard D. McCall, *Do This: Liturgy as Performance* (Notre Dame: University of Notre Dame Press, 2007), 87–88.

19. Maurice Merleau-Ponty, "Faith and Good Faith," in *Sense and Non-sense*, trans. Hubert L. Dreyfus and Patricia Allen Dreyfus (Evanston, IL: Northwestern University Press, 1964), 175.

liturgy. Here I am particularly thinking of art and its connection to the term "aesthetic." Although the discipline of aesthetics is normally considered to be a branch of philosophy concerned with art and beauty, the Greek term αἰσθάνεσθαι (*aisthanesthai*) means simply "to perceive." True, ancient Greek philosophy has been particularly concerned with beauty, but art can also be defined as having particular appeal to our aesthetic sense, which is strongly connected to our physical senses. Given that incense and music are part of every service at Saint Gregory's, as are bread and wine, one's senses are active throughout the liturgy. One does not partake in the liturgy as a disembodied mind but as a fully embodied person. The goal of a service like that of Saint Gregory's is to engage the entire person, mind and body, as I learned during a recent visit.

Upon entering the building I am greeted by Sara Miles, author of *Take This Bread*, the story of her dramatic conversion.[20] She gives me a red name tag. As I wait for the service to begin, I realize that I have never seen a worship space quite like this one. The altar—or, as the church calls it, *Jesus's Table*—is in the *back* of the church, where one enters. Again, it is clear that all are welcomed, for the inscription on the altar reads: "This Jesus welcomes sinners and eats with them." It soon becomes evident that the congregation gathers at Jesus's Table in eager anticipation of the beginning of the service. And it is there where the service begins, with a prayer, some announcements, and yet another welcome to everyone. Then the cantor (usually Sanford Dole, the music director) casually explains how the service will go. He sings the melody of the first piece of music, usually a version of the Trisagion, which may be sung in unison or in parts.[21] The music at St. Gregory's is an unusual blend of Syriac and Hebrew music, Gregorian chant, traditional Anglican music, and African American spirituals. Then the cantor previews some of the other music for the day, giving the congregation a brief chance to practice and become comfortable with the music. At Saint Gregory's, the music is sung unaccompanied by instruments. Harmony, both written and spontaneously improvised by the congregation, is encouraged. Although there is a choir, the choir members

20. Sara Miles, *Take This Bread: A Radical Conversion* (New York: Ballantine, 2007).
21. The Trisagion is sung in most Eastern Orthodox Churches. The basic phrase "Holy God, Holy and Mighty, Holy Immortal One, have mercy upon us" is normally sung three times.

are interspersed throughout the congregation—which means that wherever you're standing, nearby is a good singer whom you can count on for help. Then the cantor says, "I think we're ready to move on to the rest of the service!" Obviously, the goal is to get everyone to participate so that everyone feels comfortable becoming part of the artistic worship. So, when Sanford leads in singing, everyone follows. Even as a visitor, I felt I was a part of what was happening.

The singing that opens the service takes place while the worshipers move to the other part of the church. The procession is festive, with a raft of Ethiopian crosses. The congregation moves to seats that are arranged in two blocks that face each other in a style reminiscent of a Quaker meetinghouse. Then there are the readings. Where one would usually hear the phrase "The Word of the Lord" after the readings, instead one hears bells. Following the Gospel reading, there is an incredibly long pause that pushes the listener to respond to what has just been spoken. Even more surprising, after the relatively short sermon and a time of meditation, everyone is invited to respond by speaking up. Here again one has the impression of being in a Quaker service, in which the congregation is very much involved. And people at Saint Gregory of Nyssa's need no coaxing: they speak up immediately and take turns responding for about the same amount of time as the sermon itself. For the return to Jesus's Table, instructions are given: "Put your left hand on the right shoulder of the person to your left . . ." A visitor doesn't know that these instructions are designed to make it possible to dance back to the altar, for the word "dance" is never used. Back at the altar, the peace is exchanged and then the Eucharist is celebrated. The elements are distributed to members of the congregation, who in turn serve them to other members in such a way that one is both served and serves others. The service concludes with a hymn during which everyone joins in a Greek tavern dance. It is only after the service that I realize the significance of my red name tag: because it identifies me as a visitor, everyone involved in running the service comes up to greet me. And then suddenly those involved in the service disappear to spend five minutes discussing what went well in the service and what could be improved.

Saint Gregory of Nyssa Episcopal Church presents us with a most interesting example of liturgy. But, before we can go any further, we need to consider something quite important about the very word "liturgy." As Schmemann puts it: anyone who merely mentions the word liturgy "is likely to get involved in a controversy."[22] On the one hand, those who see themselves as attending liturgical churches often have very definite ideas of what liturgy should look and sound (and even *smell*) like. Even members of the same denomination can get very protective about their own ways of worshiping and quite critical about other ways, and members of a particular church often have very specific ideas of how the liturgy should go. The Anglican tradition is composed of liturgies that roughly can be classified as "evangelical" or "low church," "broad church," and "Anglo-Catholic" or "high church." On the other hand, people who consider their own churches to be "nonliturgical" are apt to associate "liturgy" with "smells and bells" kinds of folks. For them, "liturgy" can smack of meaningless repetition, canned prayers, and showy formality. No doubt, liturgy *can* become routine and meaningless; yet simply using a prayer book hardly means that it *must* become so. Here we need to take a closer look at the very notion of liturgy.

The word *leitourgia* is composed of two words, *leitos* and *ergon*. It is often translated as "the work [*ergon*] of the people [*leitos*]." Although we think of it as a highly specialized word, its ancient meaning is rather ordinary. We noted in the introduction that the term is used to describe how people live their lives. Roman citizens performed *leitourgia* when they paid their taxes, for they were performing a service to the state. In its religious use, the word can be translated as "public worship" or "service to God." Of course, since the Roman state was so closely connected to the Roman pagan cult, even paying taxes had religious connotations. The New Testament uses the term multiple times,[23] normally in the sense of service or ministry. For instance, Paul praises the Philippians for their ministry (λειτουργίας) to him (Phil. 2:30) and the Corinthians for their financial λειτουργίας (2 Cor. 9:12). So it is really a matter of *service* (which is why we call church meetings "worship *services*"). Yet Luke at one point uses the term in a way very close to the way we use it today, for he describes the church in Antioch as worshiping (λειτουργούντων) the Lord (Acts 13:2).

While various churches have different ways of conducting their respective liturgies, there is one aspect that unites them all. Perhaps

22. Schmemann, *For the Life of the World*, 25.
23. See Luke 1:23; Acts 13:2; 2 Cor. 9:12; Phil. 2:17, 30; Heb. 8:6; 9:21.

the most important thing we can say about liturgy is that *every church has one*. Despite the fact that people talk about "liturgical" and "nonliturgical" churches, there simply are no churches that are truly "nonliturgical." For liturgy is about what we as believers *do* when we gather together on Sunday, or at any other time during the week. The main differences between so-called liturgical churches and others is that the former normally have a long tradition of specific *practice* on which to draw. We can say that such churches are usually heavily "scripted." Anglicans have *The Book of Common Prayer*, which provides a script for most services. But even churches on the other end of the spectrum tend to have an order, and that order—in both kinds of churches—is one that both those leading and those attending often see as sacrosanct. I remember hearing the story (perhaps quite apocryphal) of a young minister of an evangelical church who was left in charge of the service one Sunday evening. Having a large number of people come forward at the altar call, he fully expected the church elder that approached him after the service to compliment him. Instead, the elder said, "If you ever move the announcements again, you're history." Talk about a strong sense of liturgy!

Worship services have different levels and different kinds of "scriptedness." One way liturgies vary is in terms of the number of items that are included. Simple services may begin with a time of singing, continue with the reading of the Word and preaching, and then end with another time of singing. More complex liturgies—in such traditions as the Anglican, Lutheran, and Roman Catholic traditions—are composed of numerous distinct parts, such as a time of gathering, reading and expounding of the Word, prayer, passing of the peace, preparing of the Eucharistic table, Great Thanksgiving, breaking of the bread and sharing of the gifts, and dismissal.[24] Each of the parts of a church service may themselves be composed of carefully scripted actions and speech. Sermons vary from being impromptu homilies ("As I was driving to church this morning . . .") to being read word for word. Prayers can be fully or partly read. In some cases, the various items of the service are printed in a book of worship. In other cases, the weekly bulletin *is* the script. Even in cases where there is no bulletin, those attending

---

24. Here I am following the order specifically set out by the Episcopal *Book of Common Prayer* (New York: Church Publishing, 1979), 401 (hereafter cited as *BCP*).

the service are usually given instructions about where to turn in their Bibles, whether to sit or stand, and what song to sing.

In general, members of so-called nonliturgical churches value spontaneity, a feeling of being fresh and authentic, since those praying, for example, are speaking from their hearts. Conversely, "liturgical" churches find the depth and richness of their prayers, which have been painstakingly written, to be preferable. But these assumptions are somewhat misleading. For example, one remarkable thing about the worship service at Saint Gregory's is that it feels so spontaneous. And yet it is actually highly scripted. In other words, it achieves what less liturgical churches often hope to achieve—a sense of openness, spontaneity, and lack of formality, and the sense that the Holy Spirit is alive in guiding the worship. But it does so by very closely following a script, one that gets modified on the basis of those short meetings after each service. On the other hand, those in the evangelical tradition know how "spontaneous" prayers can become rather predictable ("Lord, we just . . ."). Less formal churches often rely on a rather small set of worship songs that are rotated rather frequently. Many seemingly nonliturgical churches fall into rhythms that might as well be scripted simply because they vary so little.

Even though there is nothing like a schema that all churches follow, there is a general sort of pattern that many follow, whether it is fully laid out or more implicit. In technical liturgical terms, it is known as the *ordo*, which is the Latin term for "order." Dom Gregory Dix speaks of "the shape of the liturgy," and, indeed, there is a kind of "shape" or form common to many expressions of worship.[25] It is a pattern that goes back to the early church. While there are far too many specific patterns of liturgy to describe here, I will consider the various features of worship services that are common to many Christian expressions by turning explicitly to *The Book of Common Prayer*. We will see that the call and response structure that we discussed above is absolutely central to corporate liturgy.

Yet, before we turn to these specific points, it is important to note that the very "repetition" of the liturgy is always *improvisational*. That is, it is constantly being reshaped and performed anew, which should come as no surprise. Even if the celebrant is trying to follow

25. Dom Gregory Dix, *The Shape of the Liturgy*, new ed. (New York: Continuum, 2005).

the instructions "to the letter," there is still a difference between one repetition and another, in the same way that there is a difference between one performance of a symphony and another. However, this repetitive aspect presents a kind of challenge: however much one repetition might vary from another, the repetition itself can be good or bad, fruitful or simply annoying. For instance, Begbie points out that *"eucharistic repetition can 'go flat.'"*[26] It can become simply "repetitive" in the sense of being mechanical and done mindlessly. Given such a danger, it is no wonder that "nonliturgical" churches value their spontaneity. In any case, the goal is to keep the repetition fresh so that it almost seems to be the first performance. Such is the challenge of intensive liturgy.

The Call to Worship

> And on the day called Sunday all who live in cities or in the country gather together in one place.
>
> Justin Martyr, *First Apology* 67[27]

Worship begins with the call. Schmemann reminds us that liturgy—certainly that of the Eucharist or Lord's Supper—is a journey. We quite literally leave our homes and join together to *"constitute the Church."*[28] It is at this point that we separate ourselves from the world, and even this movement is itself a sacramental act. Historically, many services begin with a moment of invocation, a prayer in which we invite God to be present at the liturgy. In the Eastern Orthodox liturgy, a doxology is usually given, in which the priest says, "Blessed is the Kingdom of the Father, the Son, and the Holy Spirit, now and ever, and unto ages of ages." The standard Anglican service begins almost identically: "Blessed be God: Father, Son, and Holy Spirit," says the priest. And the people respond to the call to worship, saying, "And blessed be his kingdom, now and forever. Amen." Or consider how similar the opening was one morning that I attended Redeemer Presbyterian Church (NYC) when Psalm 95

26. Jeremy S. Begbie, *Theology, Music and Time* (Cambridge: Cambridge University Press, 2000), 168.
27. Justin Martyr was an early father of the church. His *First Apology* dates back to AD 150–55 and contains one of the best and earliest descriptions of Christian worship.
28. Schmemann, *For the Life of the World*, 27.

was used. The minister said: "Come, let us sing for joy to the Lord; let us shout aloud to the Rock of our salvation." To which the people responded, "Let us come before him with thanksgiving, and extol him with music and song." Or remember how we noted in chapter 1, the way in which the worship at Saint Sabina Roman Catholic Church began: "I was glad when they said, 'Let us go into the house of the Lord.'"

It is at this moment that we gather to *be* the body of Christ. We—God's works of art—bless God, invoke his name, and summon him to be with us. Although these are more formal ways of gathering to worship, even quite informal liturgies have this same quality. The common praise song "Here I Am to Worship" is a way of acknowledging our gathering together for the express purpose of worshiping and bowing before God. In churches that have less formal liturgies, there is a whole collection of worship songs that invoke God's name and indicate that the congregation is coming together to worship God. We, the *ekklēsia*, are gathered together, *for we are called out*. We are called to be both the icons of God (as individuals) and *the* icon of God (collectively). Thus, the very structure of the liturgy is constituted by the call and the response. As we noted in chapter 1, God's Word calls to us. In effect, the background to every service are the words "Hear, O Israel: The LORD is our God, the LORD alone" (Deut. 6:4). And the call is always intimately related to the response. As Chrétien reminds us, "Any radical thought of the call implies that the call is heard only in the response."[29] The call only has its true being in the response. Without the response, it is as if the call has not been issued. Marion puts this as follows: "As long as this call remains (at least apparently) implicit, it will remain absolutely in vain, for it will never take place, so long as it has not been explicitly heard, recognized, admitted."[30] Thus, this call is quite radical. It can only be heard if it affects us deeply. Indeed, the call must not be deflected but instead must enter us. Being called, we present ourselves by humbling ourselves before God. It is highly appropriate, then, that in the Anglican liturgy the "prayer of humble access" follows the opening lines of the service:

29. Jean-Louis Chrétien, *The Call and the Response*, trans. Anne A. Davenport (New York: Fordham University Press, 2004), 30.

30. Jean-Luc Marion, *Being Given: Toward a Phenomenology of Givenness*, trans. Jeffrey Kosky (Stanford: Stanford University Press, 2002), 286.

> Almighty God, to you all hearts are open, all desires known, and from you no secrets are hid: Cleanse the thoughts of our hearts by the inspiration of your Holy Spirit, that we may perfectly love you, and worthily magnify your holy Name; through Christ our Lord. *Amen.* (*BCP 355*)

We have been called, and that very call exposes our sinfulness in light of God's holiness. Of course, this is precisely what happens to Moses when he is confronted by the God in the burning bush: as soon as Moses says, "Here I am," God tells him to remove his sandals, for he is standing on holy ground (Exod. 3:4–5). In effect, God calls us to his holy ground.

Yet how should we think of this moment that begins the service each week? What does it mean to celebrate the liturgy each week? Are we merely repeating "the same old thing," or is something else going on? Historically, the church has understood its meetings on Sunday to be both a continuation of and likewise a break with *kronos*, or common time. On the one hand, Sunday is the first day of the week. In effect, it *frames* the week, for the week is situated between one Sunday and the next. The liturgy on Sunday provides the context for the other days of the week, reminding us that the liturgy *continues* throughout the week in the form of extensive liturgy. Yet Sunday has likewise been seen as a decisive break with common time and is thus known as "the eighth day." Gordon Lathrop puts this quite memorably when he writes that the eighth day "opens toward what cannot be reached simply by more days like those of the seven-day weeks we have known."[31] When we enter into the time of the eighth day, we move from common time to a new sort of temporality. Gadamer's reflection on the nature of "festivals" is helpful here in thinking about the temporality of the weekly service. Gadamer speaks of the "highly puzzling temporal structure" of festivals in which "every repetition is as original as the work itself."[32] Each time the liturgy is celebrated, it is as if it is being celebrated *anew*, rather than being merely repeated. The time of the liturgy is a kind of "present" that points to the past of God's redemptive work and likewise to the future of the *eschaton*.

---

31. Gordon W. Lathrop, *Holy Things: A Liturgical Theology* (Minneapolis: Fortress, 1993), 39. Those familiar with this text will note its influence upon this chapter.

32. Hans-Georg Gadamer, *Truth and Method*, trans. Joel Weinsheimer and Donald G. Marshall, 2nd rev. ed. (New York: Continuum, 1989), 122.

We are taken up and away from the normal time of everyday life into
a kind of moment that suspends time. The liturgy exists precisely
in its moment of celebration. It is when we as the *ekklēsia* gather
together that the liturgy exists. This aspect of *kairos* is even part
of the Eastern Orthodox liturgy. For, early on in the service, the
deacon says, "It is time [*kairon*] for the Lord to act." There is the
recognition, then, that the service moves us into a different dimension of time.

The festive movement that opens the service at Saint Gregory of
Nyssa's is a vivid reminder that one is entering festival time. There
are all the makings of a festival: a grand procession, multiple crosses
lifted high, and festive music sung by congregation and choir. It is
a time in which all senses are engaged by artistically crafted and
aesthetically pleasing crosses, colorful vestments, beautiful music,
incense, and dancing congregational movement from one space to
another. That movement says something like, "We are moving out
of the usual confines of the space and time continuum to a new
sense of both space and time." But festival time also means that
there is "no separation between one person and another. A festival
is an experience of community and represents community in its
most perfect form."[33] Through the liturgy, we are brought together
as one icon of the living God.

Word, Creed, and Prayer

> And the memoirs of the apostles or the writings of the prophets are
> read, as long as time permits. When the reader has finished, the ruler
> in a discourse instructs and exhorts to the imitation of these good
> things. Then we all stand up together and offer prayers.
>
>   Justin Martyr, *First Apology* 67

As is clear from Justin Martyr's account, following the gathering in the Lord's name, the early church traditionally has turned to
the reading of the Word, preaching, the reciting of the creed, and
the prayers of the people. That liturgical formula—with modifica-
tions—is still the basic formula of many churches today.

33. Hans-Georg Gadamer, "The Relevance of the Beautiful," in *The Relevance of
the Beautiful and Other Essays*, ed. Robert Bernasconi (Cambridge: Cambridge University Press, 1986), 32.

Word. It often comes as a surprise to those not familiar with more formal "liturgical" churches how much the Bible figures into their services. Normally, there is an Old Testament reading, a psalm that is either said or sung by the congregation, a New Testament reading (most likely from one of Paul's epistles), and then the Gospel reading. By comparison, in many evangelical or Pentecostal churches there is often only one Bible reading. Yet the reading of the Word—that is, the reading of the Word *aloud*—is historically a very important part of worship. Any literate person can read the text to herself, but there is something special about the *ekklēsia* gathering to hear the Word as spoken. Indeed, upon ending the reading, the reader says, "The Word of the Lord," and the congregation responds, "Thanks be to God." It is clear that something remarkable is going on in these moments in which the Word is actually being *heard* by the community of faith. The formula for the Gospel is even more elaborate. The reader says, "The Holy Gospel of our Lord Jesus Christ according to . . . ," and the people respond, "Glory to you, Lord Christ." The reader concludes with the formula, "The Gospel of the Lord," and the people respond, "Praise to you, Lord Christ." We noted that at Saint Gregory of Nyssa's they ring bells at the end of the reading—a somewhat more artistic way of saying, in effect, "Pay attention to what has just been read aloud!" Even the fact that in many traditions the Gospel is read from a beautifully bound book that is held aloft as it is carried into the service shows how art serves to intensify and beautify the moment of reading the Gospel.

While the reading of the Word is not often thought of as an artistic act, it most certainly is, in several respects. First, many of the readings are themselves narratives. To read them is to retell a story. One is not merely reading words; one is telling the story. And anyone who tells a story chooses which details to emphasize and which to exclude. At the end of his Gospel, John writes, "But there are also many other things that Jesus did; if every one of them were written down, I suppose that the world itself could not contain the books that would be written" (John 21:25). John realizes that there is much that his account leaves out. So the art of his telling of the Gospel story is figuring out what to include and how to frame it. In the next to the last chapter, John likewise writes that there were many other things he could have included; however, he goes on to say, "But these are written so that you may come to believe that Jesus

is the Messiah, the Son of God, and that through believing you may
have life in his name" (John 20:31). It is not often that storytellers are
so upfront about the purpose of their writing, but here John wants
to be crystal clear. If one compares the various Gospels, it likewise
becomes apparent that each Gospel writer has a slightly different
story to tell, and their various perspectives put together shed much
more light on Jesus's story than simply one Gospel account would
on its own. Read together, the Gospels become a beautiful mosaic
of the story of Jesus, adding and supplementing one another. They
are themselves polyphonic voices that sing together.

Second, even when the passage is not a story *itself*, the story is
always the backdrop. Much of the book of Leviticus is, to be honest, rather dry. Yet the context in which it is set is dramatic. For this
is the Word of the Lord who has brought his people out of Egypt
and is directing them to the promised land. There is an overarching story into which it fits, and that story is absolutely central to
making sense of and seeing how dynamic and powerful Leviticus
truly is. Or, to take a different example, if one considers the first
epistle to the Corinthians, there is quite a lot of intrigue at work:
a man sleeping with his stepmother, flagrant abuses of the Lord's
Supper, and a "party spirit" (no, not that kind of party but rather
the division into parties and taking sides). Thus, Paul's comments
are set in the context of what could make for a racy novel (and
the reason that we have to be so selective in what parts of the Old
Testament or Hebrew Bible are read by children is that it's filled
with stuff that is, well, rather lurid).

Third, these stories are told as a way of making our lives part of
God's overarching story so that we can become living pieces of art
that glorify God. We are asked to live the life of Jesus's kingdom.
Reading both what Jesus says about that kingdom and how his immediate followers were trying to live out that kingdom proves highly
instructive and helps us to "move into" that story—to make that
story part of *our story*. The meeting of the *ekklēsia* each Sunday
is part of that living out the kingdom. As I write this chapter, we
are in the midst of Holy Week, the climax of the church year. On
Palm Sunday, there is a dramatic difference between the first half
of the service and the second half. For the service begins with the
carrying of the palms and the celebration of Jesus's spectacular
entrance into Jerusalem. There is a dramatic reading—taken from
Scripture—that is read in many churches. It moves from the high of

Palm Sunday to the low of Good Friday. Called the "Passion Narrative," it is dramatically read aloud by a small cast representing Jesus, Peter, the chief priest, Pilate, and others. At certain points, it calls for congregational participation, especially when the entire congregation joins in shouting, "Crucify him! Crucify him!"

It should come as no surprise that the passion narratives in the Gospels are designed to be read aloud by the community of believers. So not only are the readings that are part of the service often themselves stories—and always set within the context of stories—but reading them aloud is part of the church's own story. Reading these texts is itself an art form. The reader is charged with the task of making the texts come alive, to be vibrant and fresh. It is a great responsibility.

Preaching. Even more of an art is the preaching of the Word. In chapter 3, we considered how Gadamer's notion of play is helpful in thinking about how pieces of art come into being. It is no less helpful in thinking about how homilies or sermons come into being, for they too are a kind of art. Indeed, learning the art of composing a sermon takes some doing. In my tradition, we normally have four texts (Old Testament, Psalm, New Testament, Gospel) with which to work. Often the challenge is figuring out exactly why and how the particular passages were chosen and how they might be read in tandem. Or one might, as is quite common, choose to focus on the Gospel reading. In any case, one respectfully "plays" with text, working between it and commentaries, considering what other interpreters have said, and considering how one might go in a different direction or how one might read the text in a somewhat different way. It is a type of improvisation, in which the preacher "improvises" upon the text. Jesus's own preaching evidences very much this kind of playfulness with the text. One of his constant refrains is "You have heard that it was said," followed by "But I say unto you."[34] Even though Jesus qualifies these radical statements with the statement, "Do not think that I have come to abolish the law or the prophets; I have come not to abolish but to fulfill" (Matt. 5:17), to his audience this would have sounded like a strange fulfillment indeed. And Jesus does not merely confine his improvising to the commandments of the Torah. He likewise appropriates the imagery of the Hebrew Bible for his own stories. The parable of the

34. Matt. 5 is filled with such sayings (see, for example, verses 21–22, 27–28, 31–32, 33–34, 38–39, 43–44).

vineyard (Mark 12:1–12), for example, is clearly based on the "song of the vineyard" in Isa. 5:1–7. However, while there are important points of similarity, Jesus does not merely retell the same story. Jesus's version is primarily about *himself*. Thus, Jesus—a master improviser on Old Testament texts—inscribes a new reading within an old one, affirming both but transforming the old so that it can no longer be read in the same way. The improvisation that Jesus exemplifies could be described in terms of Derrida's "iterability," which Derrida describes as "alterability of this same idealized in the singularity of the event, for instance, in this or that speech act. It entails the necessity of thinking *at once* both the rule and the event, concept and singularity."[35] Iterability is a way of thinking the universal that is always at once singular. The point of iterability is that citation is always at once repetition and transformation.[36] In effect, Jesus repeats and alters. Such is the nature of improvisation.

In preaching, one attempts to be like an icon, drawing the listener to God. In idols, we see ourselves; conversely, icons draw our attention toward God: they act as windows through which we gaze. The complication in preaching is that the one preaching is always pointing toward God, and yet human language is always inadequate

35. See Jacques Derrida, *Limited Inc* (Evanston, IL: Northwestern University Press, 1988), 119. Although Derrida explicitly works out the notion of "iterability" in "Signature Event Context" and "Limited Inc a b c . . . ," the *idea* is already present in his discussions of Husserl, particularly *Edmund Husserl's Origin of Geometry: An Introduction*, trans. John P. Leavy (Stony Brook, NY: Nicolas Hays, 1978), and *Speech and Phenomena and Other Essays on Husserl's Theory of Signs*, trans. David B. Allison (Evanston, IL: Northwestern University Press, 1973). Certainly it is connected to the notion of *différance* (and Derrida explicitly connects them in "Signature Event Context"). So we might say that the concept of iterability is an example of iterability.

36. Note that Derrida says that "everything begins with reproduction" in "Freud and the Scene of Writing," in *Writing and Difference*, trans. Alan Bass (Chicago: University of Chicago Press, 1978), 211, and likewise that "everything 'begins', then, with citation" in "Dissemination," in *Dissemination*, trans. Barbara Johnson (Chicago: University of Chicago Press, 1981), 316. Of course, one *might* argue that Jesus is simply bringing out the "real" meaning or "a" meaning of Isa. 5:1–7 that had been there all along. I find such an interpretation implausible, since Jesus's parable differs significantly from the allegory of Isa. 5:1–7.

Why this explanation is included in Matt. 21:33–46 but missing in Mark 12:1–12 and Luke 20:9–18 is for New Testament scholars to dispute. A further difference worth noting is that between the Synoptic Gospels and the *Gospel of Thomas* 93:1–16, which is free of allegorical elements. For more on this, see C. S. Mann, *Mark* (Garden City, NY: Doubleday, 1986), 455–67.

in depicting God. Thus, we point toward that which exceeds our grasp. And yet we are called to speak. In the Great Commission (Matt. 28), Jesus instructs his disciples to go forth and tell the good news. That charge is not merely to preachers but to all of us.

Creed. As is the custom in many churches, each week my church recites the Nicene Creed. The creed enunciates our core beliefs as a Christian community, giving us a chance both to remind ourselves what it is we believe and to ponder these holy mysteries. Yet the creed is itself rightly seen as embedded in the service of holy baptism. For the baptismal covenant is the moment in which we commit ourselves publicly to following God. It is a very serious moment—a *momentous* moment—in which we both renounce allegiance to Satanic forces and affirm our allegiance to God. Consider how these vows follow the pattern of call and response:

Question: Do you renounce Satan and all the spiritual forces of wickedness that rebel against God?

Answer: I renounce them.

Question: Do you renounce the evil powers of this world which corrupt and destroy the creatures of God?

Answer: I renounce them.

Question: Do you renounce all sinful desires that draw you from the love of God?

Answer: I renounce them.

Question: Do you turn to Jesus Christ and accept him as your Savior?

Answer: I do.

Question: Do you put your whole trust in his grace and love?

Answer: I do.

Question: Do you promise to follow and obey him as your Lord?

Answer: I do.

Each of these questions asks us about our direction in life. As we have seen, the very notion of *metanoia* is all about changing our life course. We *turn* to God, and in so doing turn away from the world.

Given the nature of these baptismal vows, it should come as no surprise that they naturally lead to saying the creed in the baptismal service (in this case, the Apostles' Creed). It, too, follows the call and response pattern. The congregation is asked: "Do you believe in God the Father?" In turn, the people respond: "I believe in God, the Father almighty, creator of heaven and earth." By way of question and answer, the congregation says the entire creed. Yet it does not end there: the baptismal covenant continues with various other questions, such as "Will you continue in the apostles' teaching and fellowship, in the breaking of the bread, and in the prayers?" The response is: "I will, with God's help."

Such is the liturgy for every baptism service. It is perhaps the most moving service for me precisely because of the opportunity to articulate very clearly what we believe and remind ourselves of what we renounce. Moreover, it allows us to feel particularly strongly the call and the response in which our lives and faith are so deeply embedded.

Prayer. Chrétien makes the astounding claim that "prayer is the religious phenomenon par excellence, for it is the sole human act that opens the religious dimension and never ceases to underwrite, to support, and to suffer this opening."[37] What does he mean by such a strong statement? One might first wonder if this is not far too strong a statement—prayer as the *only* way to the "religious dimension"? Yet "prayer" for Chrétien covers a multitude of acts, not simply "prayer" in its narrowest definition. Of course, prayer is possible because God first addresses *us*. We are never the initiators of a conversation with God—nor do we conclude that conversation. But clearly Chrétien also realizes that this prior address is at the heart of the structure of the call and the response—the call always preceding us. So God's speaking to us and our responding to God are not separate acts but instead go hand in hand to form a structure. It would not be inappropriate to refer to this entire structure as "prayer," for addressing God and being addressed by God are both part of prayer. Inspired by St. Bonaventure, Steven Chase considers prayer in terms of "the tree of life planted in the soul."[38] As such, the idea is that all that we do can become a part of prayer. It is not simply that we "pray without ceasing" (1 Thess. 5:17) in the usual sense of prayer, but that we also become constantly aware of God's presence and thus are always immersed in prayer.

37. Jean-Louis Chrétien, "The Wounded Word: The Phenomenology of Prayer," in *Phenomenology and the "Theological Turn": The French Debate*, ed. Dominique Janicaud (New York: Fordham University Press, 2000), 147.

38. Steven Chase, *The Tree of Life: Models of Christian Prayer* (Grand Rapids: Baker Academic, 2005), 13.

Thus, Chase wants to get beyond the "active" versus "contemplative" conception of prayer, seeing prayer as a kind of conversation that is ultimately grounded in God. Chase reminds us of the rather different Latin translation that Erasmus gives of John 1:1. Instead of "In the beginning was the Word" (*verbum*), he writes, "In the beginning was the conversation" (*sermo*), a translation certainly justified by the many meanings of the Greek word *logos* (which Erasmus is translating here). Of course, though this was forgotten by many, Erasmus was merely restoring the translation to the word originally used by the Latin Fathers. On this translation, to pray is to become part of the conversation that is Jesus Christ.

But Chrétien adds a further aspect that needs to be considered here: "Revelation"—God's speaking to us—"must shatter something in us in order to be heard. It reaches us only by wounding us."[39] Although this is rather strong talk, Chrétien is getting at something quite important. To hear God's call is to be *opened up*. Encounters with God recorded in Scripture always have this character. Think back to Moses and the burning bush: Moses has to be able to "hear" God *as* God (rather than as "talking bush"). Moreover, God calls Moses to do something that he finds remarkable, to say the least. So the call must not simply be heard; it must be *taken to heart*. To be wounded by the call is to be reminded of our unfaithfulness and our need to confess our sins and come before God with humility. It is not just the formal confession of sin in which this recognition takes place. Elsewhere, Chrétien points out that "all prayer confesses God as giver by dispossessing us of our egocentrism."[40] By its very nature, prayer requires a kind of humbling of ourselves before God. One certainly doesn't *begin* thinking of oneself as decentered, willing and ready to recognize an obligation to an other—whether human or divine. As a little child, one begins with a world in which one is the center. Or such is what one supposes. Yet, if Chrétien is right about the constitution of ourselves being so closely connected to our being constituted by others (something we noted in chapter 3), then it is really more a question of how we *think* about ourselves than how we truly *are*. To think rightly is always a struggle, though not the sort of struggle in which one finally *wins*, but rather the sort in which one continually *engages*. In that sense, all of our encounters

39. Jean-Louis Chrétien, *Lueur du secret* (Paris: L'Herne, 1985), 38.
40. Chrétien, "Wounded Word," 153.

with the other are struggles in which we are constantly *trying* to love God or our neighbors as much as we love ourselves.

And we likewise struggle with prayer in the more narrowly defined sense. "Lord, teach us to pray" (Luke 11:1). That there are likely thousands of books on prayer suggests that we are far from knowing how to pray. That we still pray the Lord's Prayer as the "default" prayer is, among other things, an indication that we haven't come up with anything better. Indeed, Thomas Merton well sums up the situation for all of us when he says, "We will never be anything else but beginners, all our life!"[41] Perhaps what we most learn when we try to pray is that, like the disciples, we don't know how. One is reminded of Augustine's remark about time in the *Confessions*: "If no one asks me, I know; if I want to explain it to someone who asks me, I do not know."[42] Of course, we usually *assume* that we know what it is to pray. But, when we start to think about what is involved in prayer, we realize that there is a multitude of questions. It is precisely because of the difficulty of prayer that certain liturgical traditions have prayers written out and then read aloud. The idea is that various people have thought long and hard about how to word a particular prayer. Moreover, there is something deeply connective in praying a prayer that has been prayed by believers for many, even hundreds of years. But there is likewise something to be said for the spontaneous sort of prayer. Of course, there is no need to *choose* one over the other. Both have their place, and one sort may be appropriate for certain occasions or even certain people. As one astute commentator has noted: "I think a lot of evangelicals have exhausted the individualized approach and find relief in the liturgical; people raised in cold liturgical traditions find relief in the warmth and informality of evangelical prayer."[43]

Eucharist

When we have finished the prayer, bread is brought and wine and water, and the ruler likewise offers up prayers and thanksgivings to

41. Thomas Merton, *Contemplative Prayer* (London: Darton, Longman & Todd, 2005), 37.

42. Augustine, *Confessions* 11.14.17.

43. Quoted in Philip Yancey, *Prayer: Does It Make Any Difference?* (Grand Rapids: Zondervan, 2006), 182.

the best of his ability, and the people assent, saying the Amen; and the distribution and the partaking of the eucharistized elements is given to each.

Justin Martyr, First Apology 67

It is not accidental that the congregation at Saint Gregory of Nyssa's dances to the altar. For dance is a way of signaling festive time. Certainly, the Eucharist—also known as the Lord's Supper, Communion, or Mass—is a time of celebration.

Central to the Eucharist are very earthy and material things: bread, wine, water. In the Eastern Orthodox liturgy, at the elevation of the bread, the priest says: "Holy things for holy people." And the people respond: "Only One is Holy, One is Lord, Jesus Christ." While there may be differences among Christian traditions as to exactly how "holy" these things are, clearly there is something sacred about them. With that recognition, we often place these holy things in holy receptacles—the paten for the bread and the chalice for the wine. But we also add things that intensify and signify the holiness of these objects. The large paschal candle that is lit on Easter signifies not merely the light of Christ but also God's presence among the Israelites as a cloud by day and a pillar of fire by night. Other candles likewise indicate the light of Christ (and, indeed, in baptism the candidate is often handed a candle with the phrase "the light of Christ"). The sanctuary lamp glows to indicate that there is consecrated bread and wine on reserve. Over the earthly elements of bread and wine, various words are said to consecrate them and, depending on one's theological tradition, either said simply to recall the importance of the elements or else to transform them in some way.

All of these holy things—including the festive and colorful vestments that some priests wear—engage our senses in a profound way. Instead of the service being merely a mental event, it becomes one that is at once mental and deeply physical. Here it is not that "art" needs to be utilized to make the service more vivid. Rather, the very things around which the service revolves are *themselves* artistic. A loaf of bread and a glass of wine *are* art objects. The Eucharist simply incorporates them and then adds further artistic elements. The result is that our whole being is engaged.

The symbolism of the Eucharist is so rich and multifaceted that we can only consider certain aspects here. First is the seemingly simple aspect of it being a *meal*. It is easy to get wrapped up in the symbolic aspect of such an act and forget how basic it truly is.[44] Eating is a vital part of our being, so bringing that aspect *to church* and making it central to worship is highly important. Although the "meal" of bread and wine has a special liturgical significance, that significance is highly intertwined with the very earthy act of simply eating and drinking. The symbolism works both ways. On the one hand, that we eat a spiritual meal in church elevates our everyday meals. There is an important sense that, whenever we gather together to eat and drink, we are commemorating this spiritual meal. On the other hand, the way an earthly meal feeds and sustains us is analogous to the way the spiritual meal feeds and sustains us. Second, and closely related, we eat this bread and drink this cup because Jesus *commands* us to do so: "Do this, as often as you drink it, in remembrance of me. For as often as you eat this bread and drink the cup, you proclaim the Lord's death until he comes" (1 Cor. 11:25b–26). It is Jesus himself who imbues these simple things with such significance. Exactly what the status of these objects is has been a subject of fierce and prolonged discussion. But, whatever view one holds, it is important to note that Jesus is quite clear about what he says. When he takes the bread and the cup, he does not say, "These are symbolic of my body" or "When you drink these, think back to this time before my death." Instead, he utters the simple, declarative statements, "This is my body" and "This is my blood" (Mark 14:22, 24). Something important must be going on here. In my tradition, we say that Christ is present in the Eucharist, though we do not speculate as to how. It is simply a holy mystery.

Third, the liturgy has the character—through and through—of a *gift*. Although most people think of the "offering" as a time of collection of money, it is more technically an offering to God of the very things that God has *given* to us. We present God with our money, as well as the bread and the wine, knowing that they are all gifts that we have received from God. We are merely giving back. Marion speaks of the one who receives a gift as "the gifted." Our very being is predicated upon the gift of life. And then all that we are and have are gifts too. Thus, we are called to participate in what is truly a holy mystery.

44. Andrew McGowan, *Ascetic Eucharists: Food and Drink in Early Christian Ritual Meals* (Oxford: Clarendon Press, 1999), 14.

Living Liturgically

Throughout this book, we have been working with the notion of living artistically. That is, we see our lives as works of art that we—working with the Holy Spirit—are constantly improvising. And, as we have already noted, there is an important link to liturgy. For liturgy isn't something we merely perform on Sunday. Even though we usually use the term to refer to what happens in church on a Sunday morning, we are called to *live* liturgically.

We have seen that liturgy was originally about how people *lived*. In other words, the term "liturgy" only gradually came to have a much more specialized meaning. Schmemann reminds us of *leitourgia*'s original meaning: "It meant an action by which a group of people become something corporately which they had not been as a mere collection of individuals—a whole greater than the sum of its parts."[45] Yet, sadly, the highly specialized use of the term has virtually overtaken the more original meaning of living life in ministry and service to God and neighbor. We should see our lives as *leitourgia*. In the introduction, we noted that J. J. von Allmen describes Jesus's own life as follows: "A superficial reading of the New Testament is sufficient to teach us that *the very life of Jesus of Nazareth is a life which is, in some sense, 'liturgical.'*" In other words, the life Jesus led was "*the* life of worship."[46] When the writer of Hebrews speaks of Jesus as "the high priest," he goes on to describe him as "a minister [λειτουργός] in the sanctuary" (Heb. 8:1–2). To be sure, Jesus's life is *perfectly* liturgical, in a way that our lives cannot be. Yet that in no way means that we cannot live our lives liturgically.

By defining liturgy this way, we go beyond the narrow idea that "liturgy" is merely something we do on Sunday morning. True, there is something quite special about the liturgy on Sunday, in which the Word is preached and the Eucharist is celebrated by the community of believers. Still, each day must be lived in a liturgical way. Each of us is called to be a "minister." Of course, these two senses of liturgy—personal living and corporate worship—are hardly at odds with one another. Indeed, each sense is absolutely

---

45. Schmemann, *For the Life of the World*, 25.

46. J. J. von Allmen, *Worship: Its Theology and Practice* (London: Lutterworth, 1965), 21, 23.

vital and reinforces the other. "Intensive liturgy" is what makes "extensive liturgy" possible. We worship God as the *ekklēsia*; the body of Christ literally comes together on Sunday morning. It is in these moments that we are released from "clock time" and enter into "festival time." That release is perhaps the most countercultural thing we as a body can do. For it is in this moment that we are affirming not the kingdoms of the world but Jesus's kingdom. We recognize that Jesus is truly Lord of lords and King of kings. We also recognize that the entire "ordering" of the world that we experience outside of the *ekklēsia* is a counter-ordering. Yet then we go out into the world to live out the liturgy. We work to *become the liturgy* in all that we do. Like Jesus, we become ministers to all those around us. We represent Christ to the world in the sense that we take the values of the *ekklēsia* and try to live them out in the world. Our goal is to become a living liturgy each day.

And this leads us back to the idea of living artistically. We opened this chapter with a quotation from Romano Guardini that is worth repeating here: "The practice of the liturgy means that by the help of grace, under the guidance of the Church, we grow into living works of art before God, with no other aim or purpose than that of living and existing in His sight."[47] Living out the liturgy is the *way* we become living pieces of art. Our ultimate goal is for our lives to *become* such beautiful pieces of art that we shine before God and the world.

Thus, each of us is an artwork in the making. Art flows from us precisely because we ourselves are works of art. Our souls and bodies are artworks that are far more fundamentally art than anything sketched on a page or painted on canvas. We are God's sculptures and we are called to join him in that task.

47. Guardini, *Spirit of the Liturgy*, 71.

Index